D0950078

Abraham Lincoln

George McGovern

Abraham
Lincoln

THE AMERICAN PRESIDENTS

ARTHUR M. SCHLESINGER, JR., AND SEAN WILENTZ

GENERAL EDITORS

Times Books

HENRY HOLT AND COMPANY · NEW YORK

Times Books
Henry Holt and Company, LLC
Publishers since 1866
175 Fifth Avenue
New York, New York 10010
www.henryholt.com

Henry Holt® is a registered trademark
of Henry Holt and Company, LLC.

Library of Congress Cataloging-in-Publication Data

McGovern, George S. (George Stanley), 1922–
    Abraham Lincoln / George S. McGovern.—1st ed.
        p.   cm.—(The American presidents)
    Includes bibliographical references and index.
    ISBN-13: 978-0-8050-8345-3
    ISBN-10: 0-8050-8345-6
    1. Lincoln, Abraham, 1809–1865.   2. Presidents—
United States—Biography.   3. United States—Politics
and government—1861–1865.   I. Title.
    E457.M45 2008
    973.7092—dc22
    [B]   2008029869

Henry Holt books are available for special promotions
and premiums. For details contact: Director, Special Markets.

First Edition 2009

Printed in the United States of America

1   3   5   7   9   10   8   6   4   2

For Eleanor

Contents

Editor's Note

THE AMERICAN PRESIDENCY

The president is the central player in the American political order. That would seem to contradict the intentions of the Founding Fathers. Remembering the horrid example of the British monarchy, they invented a separation of powers in order, as Justice Brandeis later put it, "to preclude the exercise of arbitrary power." Accordingly, they divided the government into three allegedly equal and coordinate branches—the executive, the legislative, and the judiciary.

But a system based on the tripartite separation of powers has an inherent tendency toward inertia and stalemate. One of the three branches must take the initiative if the system is to move. The executive branch alone is structurally capable of taking that initiative. The Founders must have sensed this when they accepted Alexander Hamilton's proposition in the Seventieth Federalist that "energy in the executive is a leading character in the definition of good government." They thus envisaged a strong president—but within an equally strong system of constitutional accountability. (The term *imperial presidency* arose in the 1970s to describe the situation when the balance between power and accountability is upset in favor of the executive.)

The American system of self-government thus comes to focus in the presidency—"the vital place of action in the system," as Woodrow Wilson put it. Henry Adams, himself the great-grandson and grandson of presidents as well as the most brilliant of American historians, said that the American president "resembles the commander of a ship at sea. He must have a helm to grasp, a course to steer, a port to seek." The men in the White House (thus far only men, alas) in steering their chosen courses have shaped our destiny as a nation.

Biography offers an easy education in American history, rendering the past more human, more vivid, more intimate, more accessible, more connected to ourselves. Biography reminds us that presidents are not supermen. They are human beings too, worrying about decisions, attending to wives and children, juggling balls in the air, and putting on their pants one leg at a time. Indeed, as Emerson contended, "There is properly no history; only biography."

Presidents serve us as inspirations, and they also serve us as warnings. They provide bad examples as well as good. The nation, the Supreme Court has said, has "no right to expect that it will always have wise and humane rulers, sincerely attached to the principles of the Constitution. Wicked men, ambitious of power, with hatred of liberty and contempt of law, may fill the place once occupied by Washington and Lincoln."

The men in the White House express the ideals and the values, the frailties and the flaws, of the voters who send them there. It is altogether natural that we should want to know more about the virtues and the vices of the fellows we have elected to govern us. As we know more about them, we will know more about ourselves. The French political philosopher Joseph de Maistre said, "Every nation has the government it deserves."

At the start of the twenty-first century, forty-two men have made it to the Oval Office. (George W. Bush is counted our forty-third president, because Grover Cleveland, who served non-consecutive terms, is counted twice.) Of the parade of presidents, a dozen or so lead the polls periodically conducted by historians and political scientists. What makes a great president?

Great presidents possess, or are possessed by, a vision of an ideal America. Their passion, as they grasp the helm, is to set the ship of state on the right course toward the port they seek. Great presidents also have a deep psychic connection with the needs, anxieties, dreams of people. "I do not believe," said Wilson, "that any man can lead who does not act . . . under the impulse of a profound sympathy with those whom he leads—a sympathy which is insight—an insight which is of the heart rather than of the intellect."

"All of our great presidents," said Franklin D. Roosevelt, "were leaders of thought at a time when certain ideas in the life of the nation had to be clarified." So Washington incarnated the idea of federal union, Jefferson and Jackson the idea of democracy, Lincoln union and freedom, Cleveland rugged honesty. Theodore Roosevelt and Wilson, said FDR, were both "moral leaders, each in his own way and his own time, who used the presidency as a pulpit."

To succeed, presidents not only must have a port to seek but they must convince Congress and the electorate that it is a port worth seeking. Politics in a democracy is ultimately an educational process, an adventure in persuasion and consent. Every president stands in Theodore Roosevelt's bully pulpit.

The greatest presidents in the scholars' rankings, Washington, Lincoln, and Franklin Roosevelt, were leaders who confronted and overcame the republic's greatest crises. Crisis widens presidential opportunities for bold and imaginative action. But it does not guarantee presidential greatness. The crisis of secession did not spur Buchanan or the crisis of depression spur Hoover to creative leadership. Their inadequacies in the face of crisis allowed Lincoln and the second Roosevelt to show the difference individuals make to history. Still, even in the absence of first-order crisis, forceful and persuasive presidents—Jefferson, Jackson, James K. Polk, Theodore Roosevelt, Harry Truman, John F. Kennedy, Ronald Reagan, George W. Bush—are able to impose their own priorities on the country.

The diverse drama of the presidency offers a fascinating set of tales. Biographies of American presidents constitute a chronicle of wisdom and folly, nobility and pettiness, courage and cunning, forthrightness and deceit, quarrel and consensus. The turmoil perennially swirling around the White House illuminates the heart of the American democracy.

It is the aim of the American Presidents series to present the grand panorama of our chief executives in volumes compact enough for the busy reader, lucid enough for the student, authoritative enough for the scholar. Each volume offers a distillation of character and career. I hope that these lives will give readers some understanding of the pitfalls and potentialities of the presidency and also of the responsibilities of citizenship. Truman's famous sign—"The buck stops here"—tells only half the story. Citizens cannot escape the ultimate responsibility. It is in the voting booth, not on the presidential desk, that the buck finally stops.

—Arthur M. Schlesinger, Jr.

Abraham Lincoln

Prologue

The Greatness of Lincoln

What constitutes the bulwark of our own liberty and independence? It is not our frowning battlements, our bristling sea coasts, our army and our navy . . . our defense is in the spirit which prized liberty as the heritage of all men in all lands everywhere.
—Abraham Lincoln, speech in Illinois, September 1858

Two hundred years ago Abraham Lincoln was born in a log cabin in the Kentucky wilderness. From crude, disadvantaged beginnings he somehow recognized significant capabilities within himself and nurtured a determination to succeed. He rose improbably and unevenly, becoming a clerk, surveyor, businessman, lawyer, legislator, family man, statesman, and national political figure. From the heights of presidential power and privilege he led the country through its most terrible trial of civil war. In his resolve he maintained that no state or sectional interest could break apart a Union formed in perpetuity. In his genius he transformed the bloody struggle into a second American Revolution, a "new birth of freedom" that would finally allow fulfillment of the national promise of equality for all Americans, regardless of color.

In life he was respected and ridiculed, beloved and hated; in death he was martyred. Lincoln is revered as our greatest president, but he is certainly more than that. He is an unparalleled national treasure, a legend that best represents the democratic ideal. Every generation looks to Lincoln for strength, inspiration, and wisdom. We want to know everything about him, and we wish we could be more like him. Why do we admire him so?

Abraham Lincoln was a self-made man who rose above the circumstances of his birth. The son of antislavery Baptists, reared in the backwoods of Kentucky and Indiana, he led an unpretentious and obscure early life. He knew no privilege or advantage, and was taught no life lessons except the necessity of unrelenting work. His formal education totaled just one year, but from that brief experience in the schoolroom he learned that knowledge, no matter how acquired, would be the key to improving his station in life. He never stopped reading, absorbing, analyzing, and through dogged determination he grew in wisdom and stature.

His unquenchable ambition came from within. Certainly he longed to remove himself from his father's world of drudgery and near-poverty. Perhaps he was inspired by his mother's, and then his stepmother's, gentle insistence that he could improve himself through reading, learning, and mental activity. Perhaps, too, he carried with him a measure of New England Yankee–style initiative and character and recognition of individual responsibility. Whatever the source, Lincoln was, in the words of one biographer, "the most ambitious man in the world."[1]

He learned from all of his failures—and there were many. Dissatisfied with farm life, he left his father's home for good at age twenty-one, settling in New Salem, Illinois, a tiny village that was, like him, rough, undeveloped, and facing an uncertain future. He purchased an interest in two small general stores, but chose unreliable and perhaps dishonest men for partners who left him with a staggering debt that took him years to pay. At various times he worked as a field hand, postal clerk, blacksmith, and surveyor, positions that at best brought temporary satisfaction but left him feeling unfulfilled. He was gawky, shambling, and homespun. He lacked confidence, particularly around women, and Ann Rutledge, alleged by some to be his first true love, died of typhoid in 1835. In 1832 he lost the first political contest he entered, for the Illinois state legislature.

But Lincoln would not resign himself to failure and loss; instead he learned from each experience and carried on. People, he found, liked him despite his rough exterior—or perhaps because of it. They laughed at his jokes and liked to be around him. He inspired trust. He paid his debts. He ran again for the state legislature in 1834 and was elected, and then reelected four more times. He threw himself into the study of law, spending nearly every waking moment reading and analyzing the rules of pleading and practice, and became an attorney in 1836. He earned a reputation for honesty and sincerity, and he parlayed his standing in legal circles and his political connections into election to Congress in 1846. He shook off his broken heart over the death of Ann Rutledge and in 1842 married the vivacious Mary Todd, perhaps the most enchanting young lady in Illinois, who would fuel his driving ambition.

During most of his life Lincoln suffered from recurring bouts of emotional depression or what he and his associates called "melancholy." This is a malady that can result in agonizing, even paralyzing, despair. That Lincoln was able to contain, if not conquer, this dread affliction is a huge tribute to his strength and character.

Perhaps the best account of his depression is by the historian Joshua Wolf Shenk, who wrote of Lincoln:

> He told jokes and stories at odd times—he needed the laughs, he said, for his survival. He often wept in public and recited maudlin poetry. As a young man he talked of suicide, and as he grew older, he said he saw the world as hard and grim, full of misery, made that way by fates and forces

of God. "No element of Mr. Lincoln's character," declared his colleague Henry Whitney, "was so marked, obvious and ingrained as his mysterious and profound melancholy." His law partner William Herndon said, "His melancholy dripped from him as he walked."[2]

In 1841, at the age of thirty-two, Lincoln wrote: "I am now the most miserable man living." During his days in the Illinois legislature, his friend Robert L. Wilson said that while Lincoln was often humorous and fun-loving, he once took Wilson aside to confess that he was a victim of depression so painful that he didn't dare carry a knife lest he commit suicide. Lincoln suffered grievously. It is Shenk's view that this suffering refined and strengthened Lincoln's greatness.[3]

Lincoln's obvious sadness drew his associates and many citizens to him. Given his determination to control his emotional life and to move from challenge to challenge and from battle to battle, it may well be that he converted an apparent handicap into a political asset. His sad countenance, reflecting his internal depression, doubtless touched the hearts of many voters who came to love and admire the tall, lean, sad-faced man from Illinois.

Various factors could have contributed to Lincoln's depression: heredity, deaths in the family, business failures, election defeats, even bad weather. His law partner William Herndon reported that Lincoln believed he might have contracted syphilis in 1835 or 1836. If so, this might account for some of his anxiety about marriage. Many of the men in Lincoln's time had some kind of sexually transmitted disease or feared that they did.[4]

Despite his struggle with depression, Lincoln took advantage of his opportunities. Although he served but a single term in Congress—he took the unpopular stand of opposing the war with Mexico—he reentered the political arena in 1858, challenging the feisty Stephen Douglas for the U.S. Senate. He lost the election but won the admiration of many who heard him speak passionately about the country and its future, and he most as surely caught the attention of national political leaders. Riding a wave of good publicity after a speech at New York's Cooper Union in February 1860, where he declared that "right makes might," he sensed that the time was his. His name was bandied about for the Republican presidential nomination while his Democratic opponents bickered, hopelessly splitting their party along North-South lines. Lincoln's Republican adversaries for the nomination were not as talented and well positioned, and he became the ideal compromise candidate at the party's convention. A few months later, he was elected president of a country that seemed bent on destroying itself.

As a self-made man, Lincoln had a higher view that was not constricted to his personal success. His American Dream was that all men and women should have equal opportunity to improve their lot. He believed that each American had the right to eat the bread for which he or she toiled—a controversial view, given the racial issues that divided the country. Government's role, he said, was to "elevate the conditions of men—to lift artificial weights from all shoulders—to clear the paths of laudable pursuit for all, to afford all, an unfettered start, and a fair chance, in the race of life."[5] When these paths were cleared, he believed, any man could, through diligence and dedication, become "self-made."

Lincoln was absolutely determined to preserve the Union. He was supremely committed to this goal and he vowed to accomplish it no matter how long or costly the task. At his inauguration in March 1861, he swore a sacred and solemn oath—"registered in Heaven," he said—"to preserve, protect, and defend the Constitution." By his lights this meant preserving the Union as well. Yet by the time he became president, Lincoln's conception of the Union, and of its democratic politics, was inseparable from his deep opposition to slavery—and his adamant conviction that slavery should be, as he often said, placed on the road to extinction.

Like his fellow Republicans (and unlike more radical aboli-tionists), Lincoln believed that if the slave system could be con-fined to the Southern states, it would eventually be exhausted and face economic doom. And he knew that when the free terri-tories became free states, the national political balance would shift inexorably toward freedom. Southern slaveholders denied that the federal government had the constitutional power to im-pose such a limitation on slavery's extension. Lincoln and the Re-publicans insisted that the government had that power—and declared that they intended to use it.

Lincoln ran for president in 1860 on a platform that called for slavery's limitation—no slavery in the territories. His victory on that platform was sufficient to prompt the Southern states to start seceding, one by one, as soon as Lincoln was elected. In the ensuing political crisis over secession, Lincoln made it clear that he had neither the power nor the desire to abolish slavery in the seceding states, and that he would happily allow slavery to con-tinue there if it meant saving the Union. But he made it equally clear that he would not agree to any compromise that saved the Union if it meant forcing him to abandon his pledge to restrict slavery's expansion. Lincoln's Unionism, in other words, was not unconditional with regard to slavery. On the matter of slavery's expansion, his antislavery beliefs, democratic politics, and love of the Union converged, in ways that the secessionists could not abide. And so, as he would put it in his second inaugural address, the war came.

Lincoln firmly believed that the idea of a people's democracy was civilization's greatest experiment, and if the Union were not perpetual—if dissatisfied states could leave whenever they chose—the idea of such a democracy would be reduced to an absurdity. No government had ever been assembled, Lincoln rea-soned, with a mechanism for its own destruction. In fact, seces-sion was nothing but a fiction promulgated by rebels bent on insurrection. He refused to acknowledge that the Confederacy was a legitimate nation, and therefore he would not meet with its ambassadors.

Lincoln's remarkable quality of tolerance has been a constant source of admiration for generations of Americans. His compassion touched every area of his life. He loved children and could not bear to discipline his sons. He often represented clients in court without charge because he sympathized with their situation or because he simply wanted to help out old friends. In an age of rampant hostility against foreigners, Lincoln refused to become associated with nativist political parties like the American Party, also known as the "Know-Nothings." Instead he welcomed foreigners and encouraged their participation in political and civic institutions. And he was convinced that the best way to deal with political adversaries was to apply a friendly touch, for, he believed, a man's judgment and opinions could best be reached through his heart.[6]

Lincoln knew that slavery was wrong (a belief that he inherited from his father), and when he first saw slaves in chains on a Mississippi riverboat trip he decided he would fight the practice if and when he got the chance. He did not believe that African Americans and whites ought to live as social equals, but he was unwavering in his belief that they had the same rights to live, to prosper, and to improve their lot. Though it was limited in scope, Lincoln considered the Emancipation Proclamation his greatest achievement.

He sympathized with soldiers who fought for a noble cause. He complained when his wife spent money on frivolous things—"flub-dubs," he called them—for the White House when young men had no shoes to wear into battle. He loved meeting soldiers, particularly those who had been held prisoner or had endured extreme hardship, and he could often be seen sitting under the shade trees on the White House lawn, talking with the men he admired so much. He pardoned, reprieved, or extended great leniency to hundreds of soldiers who were derelict in their duties, because he believed in giving a man a second chance. Lincoln regularly visited Washington's hospitals, and these visits with wounded soldiers lifted his spirits as much as it did theirs. His favorite unit was the Invalid Corps, made up of men whose wounds rendered them unfit for more battle service (and who already qualified for a pension) but who volunteered for security duty. And he spent more than a quarter of his presidency in residence at the Soldiers' Home in Washington, surrounding himself with disabled veterans. He personally reviewed the military commission records of more than three hundred Sioux Indians condemned to die in Minnesota, and despite extreme political pressure he reduced to thirty-eight the number of men to be executed.[7]

Lincoln sought to embrace the suffering of others rather than distance himself from it. He mourned those men who lost their lives, and as the death tolls reached unimaginable numbers, his grief became nearly unbearable. He wrote achingly beautiful letters to the mothers of fallen soldiers, with words that could only come from the heart. And he made certain that "the world would not forget" the ultimate sacrifice made by American troops at Gettysburg and other places. Amazingly, Lincoln felt no anger toward those Southerners who took up arms against their country; as misguided as they were, he was determined to "let 'em up easy" if and when the war ended.

Perhaps Lincoln's most questionable judgment during the Civil War was his suspension of the writ of habeas corpus. This important plank in the American code of justice gave a person seized and imprisoned the opportunity for a prompt court hearing to determine if he was being held lawfully and whether or not he should be released. It may seem strange that Lincoln, a thoughtful lawyer and one ordinarily dedicated to the preservation of civil rights, should have suspended, even in wartime, an important building block in the house of freedom. It is ironic that while waging a war at least in part to extend the reach of liberty, he was willing to reduce liberty in setting aside the writ of habeas corpus. And Lincoln further clouded his stature as a champion of the Bill of Rights when he ordered some newspapers critical of his policies to be closed down.

These apparent violations of the Constitution should be judged against the threat of a bloody civil war that was tearing the nation apart. A horde of Confederate spies and saboteurs were operating within the shadow of the U.S. Capitol.

The historian Mark E. Neely Jr. makes it clear that Lincoln himself believed that the arbitrary arrests without benefit of the writ of habeas corpus were essential. In a public letter dated June 12, 1863, to Erastus Corning and others, the president wrote that the time might well come "when I shall be blamed for having made too few arrests rather than too many."[8] Indeed, not only did Lincoln feel little need to justify his actions in the seizure and jailing of those he saw as lawbreakers or threats to his prosecution of the war, but there was little if any public protest from others.

Perhaps the clearest statement of Lincoln's rationale for his extralegal actions is in his own words: "As commander-in-chief of the Army and Navy, in time of war I suppose I have a right to take any measure which may best subdue the enemy." He also contended that the seceding Southern states intended to keep "on foot amongst us a most efficient corps of spies, informers, suppliers and aiders and abettors of their cause" under "cover of Liberty of speech."[9]

The foregoing arguments help us understand the extralegal actions Lincoln took during the war, but they do not fully justify his actions. The only oath an American president takes is to uphold the Constitution. This pledge holds not only during times of peace but also in wartime. Indeed, the nation may need its constitutional protections even more in times of war than in the less turbulent times of peace. Lincoln was a superb student of the law. He might have agreed with this more sober evaluation in less disruptive times. The Civil War does not stand alone in rationalizing trespasses against civil rights. War seems to pose a danger to civil justice. Consider, for example, President Franklin Roosevelt's decision in World War II to take Japanese Americans from their homes and place them in guarded holding camps far from home. This was done despite the fact that none of the people moved from their dwellings demonstrated even a hint of disloyalty toward their adopted country.

. . .

We admire Lincoln's amazing capacity to live and work with a strong sense of discipline. As an attorney he immersed himself in the nuances of the law, giving extra attention to areas in which he had little experience. When asked what made for a successful lawyer, he replied, "work, work, work is the main thing." When analyzing a legal document or written opinion, he made it a habit to read silently, then aloud to himself, and finally aloud to his partner. He liked to give himself these repetitive chances to ponder, to analyze, to critique, for he found that in that way the point would become clear in his mind. No man worked harder to make himself a success, evidenced by his practice of making grueling trips around the Illinois legal circuit, twice each year for months at a time. While Lincoln surely loved the freedom of the Illinois prairie roads and enjoyed the camaraderie of the other attorneys and judges he worked with (and, many have surmised, often needed time away from an increasingly irritable spouse), he did not look for shortcuts or make excuses to stay home: he was internally driven to do the work.

He carried this work ethic to the White House. He rose as early as 6:00 or 6:30 each morning and stayed up late, cramming as much work into the day as he could. He ate little and afforded himself few pleasures or moments of relaxation. He decided to take a hands-on approach to running the war, reading volumes on military strategy, tactics, and maneuvers to make up for his lack of military training. His attention to military detail resulted in a new, broader definition of the president as commander in chief.

Lincoln believed that cold reason and logic could overcome any deficiency and would see him through any problem. He believed that his self-discipline could set an example for the country and that his devotion to the task would ultimately provide for victory. He grew into his job as president steadily, day by day, overcoming countless frustrations and obstacles and becoming a great leader. The historian William Lee Miller wrote that Lincoln "was not born, after all, on Mount Rushmore."[10] He got there through, among other things, hard work.

Lincoln was an extremely intelligent man. He recognized that he was intellectually gifted at an early age; some argue that he even recognized a "towering genius" in himself before he left his father's home. Despite his lack of education he was seldom, if ever, intimidated—not in a courtroom, not in a political debate, not as regards any issue he faced as president. Publicly he did not boast, but privately he often told his secretaries, when questioned about the point of view of some political rivals, "I know more about that than any of them."[11] He seldom read newspaper articles or editorials, figuring the writers were less informed than he. It would be ridiculous, said some who knew him, to call him a modest man. He was supremely confident in his ability to analyze and solve any dilemma. While Lincoln relied on his cabinet for advice, he made his own decisions.

He understood the issues of the day so well that he found deeper meanings in the war that eluded others. Recognizing that the war was fought initially to preserve the Union, and later to free the slaves, he seamlessly combined the two causes into one. At Gettysburg he communicated to the nation why the tremendous sacrifice of thousands of soldiers was worthwhile: the "last full measure of devotion" would bring about a "new birth of freedom," one as important as the victories of the Revolution, and one that would endure for all time. We still marvel at the majesty and the brilliance of those words.

Lincoln was a patriot who appreciated the historical development of his country. He felt a strong sense of gratitude to the founding fathers, who had risked everything to provide for future generations. Latter-day patriots could best repay that debt, he believed, by sacrificing their time, energy, and lives to ensure that the Union would endure with freedom for all Americans. Lincoln's hero was George Washington, a man who willingly left his home and family to lead the fight for American independence against overwhelming odds. Lincoln's contemporary political idol was Henry Clay, a probusiness, prodevelopment Kentuckian who, although a slave owner, hoped that slavery would one day end. Lincoln understood that the times called for a new kind of patriot who would fight to preserve America as earnestly as the patriots of the Revolution had fought to establish it.

In a sense, Lincoln campaigned after his 1860 election as he traveled to Washington for his inauguration, appealing to the population's nationalism and drumming up support for the fight that was sure to come. He raised the flag at Philadelphia's Independence Hall, and offered some rare fighting words to inflame the passions of his audience: "It may be necessary to put the foot down firmly!" Without question his absolute resolve to preserve the Union was not merely a political position, but was born from his love of his country.

. . .

Perhaps above all else, Americans continue to admire Lincoln's sense of himself. He was a common man who rose to uncommon heights and produced uncommon accomplishments. He had a genuine rapport with the people who elected him, and he was truly appreciative of their friendship and support. He remained true to his own convictions. It bothered his wife that she was not accepted into Washington society, but he cared not at all that some politicians and newspapermen saw him as an incompetent outsider. He focused on his duty to serve his country as president, and as commander in chief, through turbulent times. He did not shirk that responsibility—as, certainly, his predecessor James Buchanan had done. He met the responsibility as he met every other challenge in his life: with clear purpose, patience, and compassion.

Lincoln remembered his roots. His real home, he knew, was back on the prairies of Illinois. His heart was there; he was happiest there; had he lived, he would have returned there. But in the vigor of his youth and prime he worked to fulfill his enormous potential, and in doing so he saved the Union from destruction and set the stage for the end of slavery.

For all his qualities, Abraham Lincoln was, of course, imperfect. He could be moody and sullen, stubborn and insensitive. Sometimes his melancholy took over, and when it did he had to battle his way through, usually alone. He kept his feelings to himself, exasperating those who loved him. Although understandable, his lifting of the right to habeas corpus and closing down several critical newspapers were at least questionable actions. But Americans, perhaps, do not want perfect heroes. We look instead for imperfect individuals who can overcome their inadequacies and accomplish great things.

Lincoln became a new kind of American hero who, in his words, stirred the "better angels" of the American people and instilled in them a passion for universal freedom. He was eulogized as one "elevated from the people, without affluence, without position, either social or political, with nothing to commend him but his own heart and sagacious mind."[12] In his greatness he remained one of us. He still is.

1

Humble Beginnings

It is difficult to make a man miserable while he feels he is worthy of himself and claims kindred to the great God who made him.

—Abraham Lincoln, Washington, D.C., 1862

Abraham Lincoln was born on Sunday, February 12, 1809, the second child and first son of Thomas and Nancy Hanks Lincoln, near Hodgenville in Hardin County, Kentucky. Thomas Lincoln's ancestors came from England and had settled first in Massachusetts in 1637. Thomas's father, also named Abraham, had been killed in an Indian attack in 1786 near Hughes Station, a fort located approximately twenty miles east of present-day Louisville. Thomas was uneducated, strong, and stocky, a carpenter and farmer by trade. Nancy was small and plain and worked occasionally as a seamstress. Her lineage is largely unknown, although some have suggested (and her son Abraham later believed) that she was born out of wedlock. The Lincoln family lived in a windowless log cabin with a dirt floor on a three-hundred-acre farm called Sinking Spring.

In 1811 Thomas moved his family to another farm near Knob

Creek, first renting and then purchasing the place for cash. Soon thereafter Nancy gave birth to another boy, this one named after his father, but he died in infancy, leaving just Abraham and his sister Sarah. It was here at Knob Creek that the children, still too young to help much with farm chores, briefly attended "ABC" school taught by teachers who were passing through. Thomas and Nancy joined the local Baptist church, and to some degree Thomas became involved in civic affairs, serving on a jury, guarding prisoners at the jail, and helping to build roads.

In December 1816 the family moved again, settling across the Ohio River on Little Pigeon Creek in Spencer County, Indiana. Thomas had no time in the winter weather to construct a decent cabin and instead threw together an open-sided shelter that was warmed only by a large fire. In the spring he cleared and planted seventeen acres with the help of Abraham, who was growing tall and strong for his age. But tragedy struck in the fall of 1818 when Nancy died of milk sickness, a condition caused by drinking the milk of cows that had eaten poisonous white snakeroot. Thomas built a coffin, and she was buried on a nearby hillside, with no minister available to preside. Abraham was nine years old, and his mother's death struck a hard blow.

Thomas quickly remarried, to Sarah Bush Johnston, a woman he had known in childhood, now widowed with three children. Abraham and Sarah were happy to have new siblings, and the new Mrs. Lincoln immediately set about turning the ramshackle cabin into a home. She brought a sense of order to it, cleaned it, and had Thomas install a floor and windows and complete the roof. More important, she became very close to Abraham and quickly became his biggest influence. She recognized how eagerly he wanted to learn and she gave him some of her books, *Aesop's Fables*, *The Pilgrim's Progress*, *Robinson Crusoe*, and *Webster's Speller* among them. She understood that Abraham had little use for farm life and encouraged him to develop his intellect and attend school whenever possible. She came to love Abraham as much as or more than her own children. "Abe was the best boy I ever saw," she said many years later. "He never gave me a cross word or look and never refused, in fact or even in appearance, to do anything I requested him."[1] Abraham clearly blossomed under her love and later said that "she had been his best friend in the world and no Son could love a Mother more than he loved her."[2]

It was a different story, however, between father and son. A gulf began to separate the two. Thomas grudgingly accepted that Abraham wanted to expand his mind, but he could not understand why he shirked his chores. Abraham had no further use for splitting rails, clearing land, or plowing corn, for although his father taught him to work hard "he never learned me to love it."[3] Thomas believed his son was lazy, and many of the neighbors, to whom Abraham was hired out to work, agreed. At times Thomas became so frustrated with Abraham's attitude that he was physically abusive toward his son. As Abraham approached his eighteenth birthday, he grew more distant from his father, and he looked forward to the day when he could leave. The historian William Gienapp describes the young man's state of mind:

> In the meantime he developed at his own speed, forging traits that would remain with him his entire life. Though his parents regularly attended the Little Pigeon Baptist Church, for example, Lincoln saw no use in organized religion and shunned even the frontier revivalism that was popular. Breaking from the norms of backwoods cultural expectations he did not fight, gamble, swear or use tobacco. He disliked violence and did not hunt or fish. He took odd jobs where he had to slaughter hogs, but after once shooting a wild turkey he "has never since pulled a trigger on any larger game."[4]

In his late teens Lincoln began cautiously to test the road ahead. He traveled around the county attending barn raisings, corn shuckings, and other community events. He liked to tell stories and make jokes, and he quickly gained in popularity among the young men his age. With his cousin Dennis Hanks he sawed logs and sold firewood to steamships on the Ohio River, helped run a ferry across the river, and built fences for neighbors. Sometimes he helped out at a general store or worked for a local blacksmith. In the spring and summer of 1828 a businessman named James Gentry hired Lincoln and Hanks to pilot a flatboat loaded with provisions down the Mississippi River to New Orleans. The two boys were accosted by a group of black men at one stop along the way, but they managed to fight off the attackers and escape with their cargo intact. They got a glimpse of city life in New Orleans, and watched as large numbers of slaves were auctioned. Safely back home again in Indiana, Lincoln turned over his earnings of $25 to his father, as he was legally bound to do.

Early in 1830 Thomas felt the urge to move again, still farther westward to Macon County, Illinois, on the north side of the Sangamon River. Once again the Lincolns hurriedly built a cabin, cleared land, and planted their crops. A few months later, when his father decided to move yet again to Coles County, Lincoln, now twenty-one, did not go with the family. Instead he left his father's home, and his father's way of life, for good.

Teaming up again with Dennis Hanks and John Johnston, his stepbrother, he made his way to Springfield, the largest town in the region. There the young men met up with an energetic business-man named Denton Offutt, who hired them to build a flatboat and load it with pork barrels, corn, and hogs to be transported to New Orleans and sold at market. Just twenty miles downriver, however, the flatboat became lodged on a flooded milldam that served the tiny village of New Salem. As the townspeople watched and cheered, Lincoln cleverly maneuvered the boat out of its predicament and saved the cargo. Offutt was so impressed that he offered Lincoln a job running a general store that he planned to build in New Salem. This prospect appealed to Lincoln, and a few months later, after the successful trip to New Orleans, Lincoln reappeared in town, anxious to begin life on his own terms.

In New Salem he found a town of about one hundred people scattered atop the bluff that looked out over the Sangamon River. There were fifteen or twenty cabins, a blacksmith, a livery, a gristmill, and a few stores and taverns. Having already made a favorable impression with his skills as a river pilot, Lincoln quickly became the favorite of most of the townspeople. He was, even by frontier standards, quite a sight. Gangly and awkward, he dressed almost comically in boots, a woolen shirt, and linen pants that rose to midcalf. He talked with a nasal Southern twang, indifferent to the many words he mispronounced. He was, according to one who knew him, "about as ruff a specimen of humanity that could be found."[5] He had also stretched to his full height of six feet four inches, and at just over two hundred pounds he was lean, strong, and sinewy.

It was his physical prowess that helped gain him good standing in town. He squared off in a wrestling match with a young tough named Jack Armstrong, leader of a rowdy group known as the Clary's Grove boys. As the crowd looked on, cheering and wagering "money, whiskey and knives," Lincoln and Armstrong tussled, but neither man could throw the other. Finally, according to some, Armstrong took Lincoln down with an illegal move. The match was over, but Lincoln proved the good sport, and "laughed the matter off so pleasantly that he gained the good will of the roughs and was never disturbed by them."[6] In fact, Lincoln became good friends with Armstrong and his wife, Hannah, and the paths of the two men would cross regularly over the years. Lincoln's performance in the match won him the admiration of the town and helped him become its leading figure.[7]

New Salem took Lincoln to heart. His new neighbors loved his affable, easygoing ways. He was funny, cheerful, and kind. His honesty was a trait that particularly stood out: he was always named judge of horse races or athletic contests. There was a rough charisma to him, and he found himself the center of every crowd. Always more comfortable among men, he entertained constantly with his stories and commentaries about local affairs. He was generally bashful with ladies, and he took care to tone down his humor when he was around them. As popular as he was, however, it took some time before Lincoln found his way. He was, he later said, "a piece of floating driftwood" those first few years in New Salem.[8] He hired himself out as a field hand, split rails, and mended fences. He worked on and off at the blacksmith shop, the gristmill, and Denton Offutt's store, where he slept in the back room. Occasionally he hauled freight on the river. He became friends with the Rutledge family, one of the first to settle New Salem, and worked at the tavern and store that they owned. He also worked as a clerk for a local election board, enjoying the job immensely because it gave him the opportunity to converse and joke with the voters who came by.

His intellect was noted by many. People saw a special quality in this rough-hewn young man; he was particularly quick-witted and eager to learn. He had an analytical mind that seemed to be working nonstop. Occasionally the town schoolmaster, Mentor Graham, taught him and noted that Lincoln was "regular in his habits punctual in doing anything that he promised or agreed to his method of doing *any* thing was very systematic."[9] Remarkably, New Salem had a debating society, which Lincoln quickly joined. He began to polish his skills of elocution, and, just as important, he met people who had books he could borrow. He read at every spare moment, growing especially attached to the works of Shakespeare and Robert Burns. Bowling Green, the town's justice of the peace, lent him a copy of the *Revised Laws of Illinois*, and he purchased a tattered volume of Blackstone's *Commentaries*. Green allowed him to appear informally in court and offer opinions on a few insignificant issues, and on one occasion he traveled to Boone, Indiana, to listen to the acclaimed attorney John Brackenridge argue on behalf of a client charged with murder. Lincoln insisted on shaking Brackenridge's hand, and later said, "I felt that if I could ever make as good a speech as that my soul would be satisfied."[10] Inspired by these episodes, he began for the first time to think seriously about the law. Perhaps he could use his mind and forensic skill, he thought, to advance his position in society.

Politics presented an opportunity. The residents of New Salem had always believed that prosperity would come to the town if the Sangamon River were improved so as to ease navigation, providing natural commercial routes to the Illinois and Mississippi rivers. But a strong voice was needed in the state legislature to advance New Salem's interests. Though he had lived in New Salem for less than a year, Abraham Lincoln seemed a natural choice. In March 1832 he announced his candidacy by publishing a letter in Springfield's *Sangamo Journal*.

The election, however, was still months away. In the interim, Offutt's store failed, and Lincoln again scrambled for work. His next employment came unexpectedly. Black Hawk, the elderly chief of the Sauk Indians, violated a treaty by leading twelve hundred of his people across the Mississippi River into Illinois in search of land suitable for planting corn. Governor John Reynolds called for volunteers to suppress the "insurrection," and Lincoln quickly mustered in. Along with other men, many from New Salem, they formed a company at Richland, and to his delight Lincoln was elected captain. He immediately named Jack Armstrong his first sergeant.

Lincoln had no military experience, but as it turned out none was needed. The ragtag group tramped about the Illinois countryside for a month or so, then made their way north to Wisconsin, but saw no sign of the elusive Black Hawk. Later Lincoln joked about his military adventures, stating that "he fought his way through hordes of mosquitoes," but actually he took pride in his short stint as a soldier.

Lincoln arrived back in New Salem just two weeks before the election. He had no time for real campaigning, but he did make a few appearances around the region, delivering the same brief speech:

> Fellow citizens, I presume you all know who I am. I am humble Abraham Lincoln. I have been solicited by many friends to become a candidate for the Legislature. My politics are short and sweet, like the old woman's dance. I am in favor of a national bank. I am in favor of the internal improvement system and a high protective tariff. These are my sentiments and political principles. If elected I shall be thankful; if not it will be all the same.[11]

Lincoln finished eighth out of thirteen candidates, with the top four going to the legislature. The defeat, he later remarked, was "the only time I was ever beaten on a direct vote of the people."[12] He was cheered, however, by his showing in the New Salem precinct, where he received 277 out of 300 votes cast.

Lincoln had to wait two more years until the next general election. In the meantime he opened a store with a man named William Berry, but Berry drank up a good share of the profits and the enterprise failed. Fortunately, Lincoln also fell into a couple of political appointments. First, he was named postmaster of New Salem, a job that gave him plenty of free time to read and converse with customers, since the mail arrived only twice a week. Although Lincoln had opposed the election of Andrew Jackson, the postal appointment was considered too unimportant to warrant patronage concerns. Then Lincoln landed a job as deputy county surveyor. He purchased the necessary tools and went at the work in earnest, platting out river courses and small area towns. He may have noted as well that his hero George Washington had also been a surveyor. These two positions kept Lincoln afloat financially until the next general election. When that election came in 1834, he was elected to the Illinois House of Representatives, finishing second out of thirteen candidates from Sangamon County. It was the first of four consecutive victories.

From the outset of his political career, Lincoln was solidly entrenched in the Whig Party, which, along with the Democrats, was one of the country's two major parties. Under the leadership of the Kentuckian Henry Clay, the Whigs espoused the idea of governmental aid to internal projects such as improved railroads, bridges, canals, and navigation systems. Pragmatically, Lincoln believed that these programs would surely help develop the West. Democrats were not on principle opposed to federally funded projects, so long as they were of genuine use to the entire nation; nor were they opposed on principle to state or local aid to state and local projects. On a personal level, Lincoln believed that the Whig Party characterized his idea of a more productive, civilized life. His rejection of his father's frontier lifestyle, his resolve to develop his talents and abilities—to become a self-made man—and even his aversion to violence, alcohol, and tobacco reflected the sort of dedication and discipline that the Whig Party favored. Lincoln's connection to the Whig Party was born from his desire to live a better life than his father had.

In 1834 the Illinois capital was Vandalia, a two-day carriage ride from New Salem. Whigs were in the minority in the fifty-five-member House, but Lincoln found a small, dedicated group of men who shared his principles and beliefs. He roomed with a Springfield lawyer named John T. Stuart, whom he had had known from the Black Hawk War. Stuart was an experienced legislator who showed Lincoln around the capital and helped him learn proper legislative procedure; perhaps more important, he lent Lincoln some law books and encouraged more self-study. Lincoln enjoyed his first term in the House, although he found himself often voting in the minority, because his easygoing ways quickly earned him friends. He was "raw-boned, angular, features deeply furrowed, ungraceful, almost uncouth . . . and yet there was a magnetism and dash about the man that made him a universal favorite," a colleague said.[13] When the session ended in February 1835, Lincoln collected $358 for salary and expenses and headed back to New Salem.

He took Stuart's advice and immersed himself in the study of law. Friends and associates in New Salem noticed that he was still constantly reading—but now his reading had a singular purpose: preparing him to become an attorney. He devoured Chitty's *Pleadings*, Greenleaf's *Evidence*, and Story's *Equity Jurisprudence*, all standard legal texts of the day. He would be admitted to the bar in March 1836.

But there was heartache in Lincoln's life before that day came. In the spring and summer of 1835 typhoid fever spread through central Illinois. One of those who died was Ann Rutledge, the bright, attractive daughter of community leader James Rutledge. Lincoln and Ann had developed a relationship in recent months. Some later said that they were to be engaged when Lincoln finished his law studies, but on August 25 Ann died of fever, and Lincoln fell into a relatively severe depression. "It was evident that he was very much distressed," recalled one neighbor. Another said that "after this Event he seemed quite *changed*, he seemed *Retired*, & loved *Solitude*, he seemed wrapped in *profound thought*, *indifferent*, to transpiring Events, had but Little to say, . . . this gloom seemed to deepen for some time, so as to give anxiety to his friends in regard to his mind."[14] Taken in by Bowling Green, he emerged from his depression, but remained "quite melancholy for months."[15] Indeed, Lincoln would struggle with these feelings sporadically for the rest of his life.

But he persevered. After a lackluster special legislative session that winter, he enjoyed a more productive session in 1836, and in the August election he received more votes than any other candidate in Sangamon County. He was named chairman of the powerful finance committee, a reflection of his growing stature in Illinois, and led a successful effort to move the capital from Van-

dalia to Springfield. Along with a fiery, ambitious Chicago Democrat named Stephen A. Douglas, Lincoln also strongly supported
the Internal Improvements Act, a series of measures designed to
bolster the state's railroad and canal systems. During the session
Lincoln also made, for the first time, official comments regarding
slavery. When a resolution was proposed condemning abolitionist
societies and affirming that slavery was constitutionally guaranteed, Lincoln refused to endorse it. Instead, he suggested that
"the Congress of the United States has no power, under the constitution, to interfere with the institution of slavery in the different states . . . the institution of slavery is founded on both
injustice and bad policy; but the promulgation of abolition doc-
trines tends rather to increase than to abate its evils."[16]

After the session Lincoln returned to New Salem, but only to
say good-bye. All efforts to improve the Sangamon River having
failed, the village was dying. Many of Lincoln's friends had moved
elsewhere, and those that remained, Lincoln knew, could not support a law practice. He borrowed a horse from Bowling Green
and stuffed everything he owned into some saddlebags, and on
April 17, 1837, with seven dollars in his pocket (the proceeds of
the sale of his surveying equipment), Lincoln rode to Springfield,
twenty miles away.

Springfield was a lively community of nearly fifteen hundred
people. Lincoln took a room above Joshua Speed's general store,
and quickly the two men, both ambitious but insecure, became
the closest of friends, sharing confidences and aspirations. Lincoln also accepted John Stuart's offer to join his law practice. The
office was located downtown, on the north side of the public
square. For the next four years Stuart and Lincoln operated a
thriving practice, the heart of which was the Eighth Judicial Circuit, a seventeen-county region in the center of the state. Twice
each year, in the spring and again in the fall, Lincoln joined a traveling caravan of attorneys and judges, stopping for a few days at
each county seat in the circuit, "bringing justice to the people."[17]

The groups stayed in inns or taverns, eating and sleeping together, then rising early for a full day at the local courthouse. Often the attorneys met their clients just a few minutes before the case was called. Lincoln, like all the others, took cases in divorce, custody, trespass, probate, and plenty of criminal defense matters. The hours were long, and the traveling, particularly in bad weather, was grueling, but Lincoln loved riding the circuit, as it was called. He honed his craft, he enjoyed the camaraderie of fellow professionals, and he particularly reveled in getting to know the people from all across the state. In time he gained a reputation as an honest, conscientious attorney in courtrooms and communities across Illinois.

Lincoln also gained a measure of acceptance in Springfield's social scene. He became a regular guest at the hilltop mansion of Ninian and Elizabeth Todd Edwards and began to mingle with the upper crust of Springfield society. Soon he made the acquaintance of Mrs. Edwards's vivacious younger sister, Mary Todd. The lovely product of a wealthy Kentucky family, at twenty-two years of age Mary was educated, witty, and opinionated. She was also charming and flirtatious, and she quickly "became the young belle of the town, leading the young men of the town a merry dance," according to one observer.[18] Said another, "She was the very creature of excitement."[19] Even Mary's brother-in-law said, "She could make a bishop forget his prayers."[20]

While Mary had her pick of all those Springfield men who flocked around her, she was attracted to Abraham Lincoln for his gentle style, his sincerity of affection, and his ability to remain humble yet confident. She looked past his crude manners and saw great possibilities. He, in turn, was fascinated by her beauty and equally impressed with her intellect. She spoke several languages and could discuss current events and politics as intelligently as fashion and design. They became a couple, spending hours chatting on the horsehair sofa in the Edwards home, taking carriage rides into the country, and attending Springfield social events. By the fall of 1840 they were engaged to be married.

But all manner of troubles arose that winter. Lincoln was fatigued from a backbreaking schedule of circuit riding, Supreme Court appearances, and legislative concerns. He and Mary quarreled, perhaps over Mary's flirtations with other men; perhaps because his self-doubts began to creep in, and he was not convinced he could satisfactorily support a wife, financially or emotionally or both; perhaps even because Lincoln was attracted to another woman. (Some historians have suggested that Lincoln loved Matilda Edwards, who did not return his feelings of affection.) For some or all of these reasons, on New Year's Day, 1841—"the fatal first of Jany.," as Lincoln later called it—things became too much for him to bear. On or around that day the engagement was called off.[21]

And now Lincoln fell into his second emotional breakdown, or serious depression. He took to his bed, and then dragged himself to a local physician, Henry Anson, who diagnosed anxiety and exhaustion. Lincoln was ineffective in the legislature, missing roll calls and votes. His condition was big news in Springfield. "We have been very much distressed on Mr. Lincoln's account," wrote one woman. "Poor L!" wrote James Conklin, an attorney, "how are the mighty fallen! . . . His case at present is truly deplorable." Speed later recalled that he had to take Lincoln's knives and razors away from him, and Ninian Edwards reported him "Crazy as a *Loon*."[22] His mental health status even made the newspapers: the Democratic Springfield *Register* poked fun at Lincoln's "indisposition."[23]

"I must die or be better," Lincoln had written. He chose to get better, but it was a struggle to rebound from the terrible winter of 1840–41. He remained moody and melancholy for months. When the legislative session ended in early March, Lincoln took some time off from the circuit to clear his head. In the summer he visited the Speed family plantation in Kentucky and came back much refreshed. He was heartened when Speed introduced him to Fanny Henning, the young lady whom, with Lincoln's encouragement,

Speed would eventually marry. Perhaps, Lincoln thought, there was reason to hope that he too could find a measure of personal happiness with a woman.

But was Mary Todd the woman? Lincoln returned to Springfield, but not to the social scene. Mary was content, it seemed, to wait for Lincoln to come around; in her letters to friends she wrote that while Lincoln "deems me unworthy of notice . . . yet I would that the case were different, that he would once again resume his Station in Society . . . much happiness would it afford me."[24] Her patience paid off. Lincoln resolved his issues of self-doubt and was also assured by Speed that married life was satisfying and fulfilling. Encouraged to "be friends again," Lincoln and Mary resumed their meetings, and found that their mutual attraction had not altogether faded. They resolved their differences and began to make plans for the future. On November 4, 1842, they were wed in a private ceremony at her sister's house in Springfield. Lincoln was nearly thirty-four years old, ten years older than his bride. Inscribed on the inside of the gold wedding band he gave her were the words "Love Is Eternal."

Lincoln set about in earnest to provide for his wife and soon-to-be family (their first son, Robert Todd, would be born in 1843, followed by Edward in 1846, William in 1850, and Thomas in 1853). Now in law practice with the former judge Stephen T. Logan, Lincoln paid more attention to detail, organization, and discipline. Logan, like so many others, saw in Lincoln a tremendous potential and challenged him to meet it. Logan became a mentor for Lincoln and as senior partner managed the day-to-day operation of the practice while Lincoln traveled the circuit and sharpened his skills. He left elected office but became involved in Springfield civic affairs, enjoying his prominence and financial well-being and earning a reputation as a member of one of the state's finest law firms. In 1844 the Lincolns purchased a house at Eighth and Jackson streets, not far from the downtown office and courthouse, where they would live for the next seventeen years.

That same year Lincoln, tired of junior partner status, was feeling confident enough to leave Logan's office. He chose for a new partner William Herndon, who had once served as his law clerk and who was something of a celebrity in Springfield because of his loud, expressive ways. Despite his youth—Herndon was nine years younger than Lincoln—and the fact that he was untried as a lawyer, Lincoln liked the enthusiasm and optimism of the youthful attorney. He trusted him completely, and the two men operated on a handshake agreement. Herndon was happy to manage the office while Lincoln was out on the circuit, where he found increasing respite from a home life that was all too often chaotic and tense.

Mary was lonely when her husband was away and impatient when he was home. She tried, with minimal success, to refine her husband by improving his dress and manners, but Lincoln remained, for all his success, at times distant, brooding, and self-contained. Mary became increasingly ill-tempered, and her physical ailments, real and imagined, increased her irritability. She argued with the neighbors and with the maids, and it was often left to Lincoln to smooth things over, which he usually did with humor and resignation.

Despite their problems, however, the Lincolns remained devoted to each other. For the most part they continued to enjoy each other's company. They delighted in spoiling the children. The Lincolns appreciated the income that the law practice produced, adding on to their house and maintaining, at least by Springfield standards, a high standard of living. Mary's confidence in her husband never faltered. Although his state political career had wound down with the Whig Party hopelessly stuck in minority status, Lincoln followed state and national politics closely, and he believed—and his wife concurred—that the chance to make his mark might come around again.

2

The Making of a Statesman

You may fool all of the people some of the time; you can even fool some of the people all the time; but you can't fool all the people all of the time.
—Abraham Lincoln, in conversation at the White House

Abraham Lincoln was a political man. Today we picture him as a sober, serious-minded statesman of the highest order, but he was also a shrewd, masterful politician who knew and appreciated the tactical and strategic demands of down-to-earth politics. He was a passionate member of the Whig Party, which had been founded in 1833 to oppose the policies of the "malignant tyrant" Andrew Jackson.[1] Mingling his law practice with politics, he became the party's workhorse in Illinois, relentlessly organizing, strategizing, and campaigning. Always stressing the necessity of proper order and procedure, Lincoln constructed a plan that organized Whigs down to the precinct level and established a state convention system that nominated candidates for state and national offices. He acted as the party's point man at rallies, fairs, and festivals "from the Wabash to the Mississippi," promoting the Whig agenda of development and populism, railing against the alleged corruption of the Jackson and Van Buren administrations. He frequently referred to Democrats as radicals who were out of the mainstream of American politics.[2] Lincoln was convinced that party unity was the key to success, advising colleagues that "a house divided against itself cannot stand," a biblical phrase he would use again in years to come. He fostered that unity by writing letters, meeting with party officials, and smoothing over internal disagreements, "willingly subordinating his own ambitions to party harmony,"[3] in the words of the historian Joel Silbey.

As dedicated as he was to the Whig Party, Lincoln also believed that his efforts would pay off for him personally, for he was fiercely ambitious. "Now if you should hear any one say that Lincoln don't want to go to Congress, I wish you . . . would tell him . . . he is mistaken," he wrote to a friend. "The truth is, I would like to go very much."[4] In 1842 he sought the Whig nomination for the newly established Seventh District of central Illinois, opposing fellow attorneys John J. Hardin (who happened to be Mary's cousin) and Edward Baker, a close personal friend. But Hardin secured the spot and was later elected to Congress. Anxious to avoid further friction within the party, Lincoln forged a unique compromise. In the future, the three candidates would serve the district on a rotation plan: after Hardin, Baker and then Lincoln would seek the party's nomination. In the interim Lincoln practiced law, kept current with his political contacts around the state and the country, and stumped for Henry Clay in his unsuccessful presidential campaign bid of 1844.

In 1846 Lincoln took his turn and defeated a revivalist Methodist preacher named Peter Cartwright in the general election. Lincoln won easily, collecting nearly 60 percent of the vote, but the race was notable because Lincoln, for the first time, set forth his religious views. Responding to charges that he was an infidel, Lincoln wrote, "That I am not a member of any Christian Church is true, but I have never denied the truth of the Scriptures." Perhaps meaning to acknowledge the popularity of evangelical

Protestantism, which had appeared on the American landscape in the so-called Second Great Awakening, Lincoln wrote, "I do not think I could myself be brought to support a man for office whom I knew to be an open enemy of, and scoffer at, religion."[5]

Larger issues loomed. Taking his seat in Washington in December 1847, Lincoln found that the Whig Party, though it held a slim majority in the House of Representatives, was floundering. Its traditional arguments for a strong protective tariff and national bank seemed as outdated as their elderly party leaders Henry Clay and Daniel Webster. President James Polk vetoed a Whig-sponsored federal improvements bill, which could not be revived. (Polk believed that internal improvements could be made only through constitutional amendment, an idea Lincoln found preposterous.) Polk's Democratic administration was popular, particularly since the army, under Generals Winfield Scott and Zachary Taylor, was scoring impressive victories in the war with Mexico, and the chances for American expansion into the California and New Mexico territories seemed promising. Following party lines, Lincoln opposed the war, carefully voting to fund the troops but questioning whether the war itself was necessary and whether America had in fact been the aggressor. He argued that the president had no power to wage war under the Constitution, for that was exclusively within the province of Congress. Further, Lincoln asserted that true title to the disputed lands in Mexico depended upon whether the inhabitants therein had revolted against their government. "Any people anywhere," he said on the floor of the House, ". . . have the *right* to rise up, and shake off the existing government, and form a new one that suits them better. . . . This is a most valuable,—a most sacred right."[6] All of Lincoln's arguments fell on deaf ears, and all would come back to haunt him when he became president.

Hoping to embarrass President Polk, Lincoln introduced the "Spot Resolutions" in January 1848, demanding that the president prove specifically where the first American had shed his

blood. This was a matter of some controversy, because it was un-
clear whether the first skirmish had occurred on American or
Mexican soil. But Polk ignored the first-term congressman, and
the House neither debated nor adopted Lincoln's resolutions.
Lincoln was disappointed to learn that his position on the war
was seen by some, even back home in Springfield, as unpatriotic.
Billy Herndon privately worried that Lincoln's political career
had been ruined.

In the spring Lincoln looked to repair the damage he feared he
had inflicted on the party. He attended the national Whig convention in Philadelphia and, working alongside a Georgia Whig
named Alexander Stephens, helped to secure the nomination of
Zachary Taylor for president; he believed that the war hero (who
had no political experience) would make a viable candidate. Lincoln advised Taylor not to interfere with the sectional interests
that were percolating throughout the country, most notably the
divisive issues of nativism and slavery in the new territories. Lincoln campaigned vigorously for Taylor in the fall, editing a Whig
newspaper and making speeches in New England. He sent out
thousands of copies of those speeches to constituents in Illinois.
Lincoln was pleased when Taylor was elected, but disappointed
when he did not carry Illinois. Even worse, the Whigs lost Lincoln's seat in Congress to a Democrat named Thomas Harris, who
effectively campaigned against Whigs who, like Lincoln, were
seen as soft on the war.

Lincoln's second, and last, year of his congressional term was
dominated by slavery. He was naturally antislavery, but he was
not an abolitionist. He firmly believed that slavery in the various
states was protected by the Constitution, and that Congress had
no power to interfere with it there. But he did seek to end slavery
in the District of Columbia, believing that slavery was a monstrous embarrassment to the nation's capital. Two thousand slaves
resided there, and it was a cruel irony that the country's largest
slave trading warehouse—"a sort of Negro livery-stable," Lincoln

called it—operated just blocks from the Capitol.[7] But Lincoln knew that the issue was explosive politically, particularly for the Whigs, whose members were divided: many in the Northeast were strong abolitionists; others were upset with the nomination of Taylor over Henry Clay; some in the South, like Alexander Stephens, were concerned that antislavery voices would inflame sectional differences. Concerned that disruption in the Whig Party would undermine the efforts of President Taylor's incoming administration (Taylor would not take office until after the session of Congress was over), Lincoln worked quietly behind the scenes to build a consensus that might satisfy everyone.

Though he gained some initial support, his modest scheme for compensated emancipation in the Federal District was doomed to fail. Senator John C. Calhoun of South Carolina, perhaps the strongest voice for slavery and states' rights, lobbied hard against Lincoln's proposal, believing that it was a first step toward nationwide abolition. Northern antislavery men also balked, believing that monetary payments to slaveholders would only legitimize the slave industry, and others opposed any measure that endorsed the fugitive slave laws. Lincoln had no choice but to abandon his proposal, and he never formally introduced the bill. He also had learned a painful lesson in politics, and saw that the differences within his beloved Whig Party might not be settled. His ineffectual two-year term in Congress at an end, Lincoln trudged back to Springfield. He wrote forlornly to a friend that "I neither expect, seek, or deserve" to return to Washington. Thus ended his single term in Congress.

Now the legal profession "superseded the thought of politics" in Lincoln's mind, and he dedicated his efforts to rebuilding his law practice. Once again he made his regular rounds on the Eighth Circuit while Herndon looked after things in the Springfield office. He enjoyed the friendship and commanded the respect of other leading figures in the Illinois bar, men such as Leonard Swett, Ward Hill Lamon, and Judge David Davis, all men who would play prominent roles in his rise to the presidency. Mostly on the strength of Lincoln's reputation and acumen, the firm built a strong base across Illinois and the Midwest, with such notable clients as the Illinois Central and Rock Island & Pacific railroads. Taking cases in admiralty, commerce, criminal, and patent law, Lincoln was so highly regarded that he was occasionally asked to serve as a special prosecutor and even as a judge. He was active in the state and federal courts, and argued before the United States Supreme Court on three occasions. By the mid-1850s Lincoln was perhaps the most respected attorney in Illinois.[8]

But politically things looked bleak, and Lincoln could only watch as the Whig Party sputtered toward oblivion. He endorsed General Winfield Scott for president in 1852 (Taylor had died in office and been succeeded by the unpopular Millard Fillmore), but he knew Scott's candidacy was doomed from the start because of division within the party. Perhaps still disillusioned by his experiences in Congress, Lincoln campaigned for Scott unenthusiastically. At the same time a new political organization, the American Party, or "Know-Nothings," emerged, an antiforeign, anti-Catholic group formed in response to rising numbers of immigrants from Ireland and Germany. Increasing numbers of disgruntled Whigs joined the movement, but Lincoln could not bring himself to acknowledge that his party was on its last legs and refused to consider joining another. In the November election, Scott was defeated by the Democratic candidate, Franklin Pierce.

The slavery issue—particularly, whether the institution should be allowed to spread into the territories—continued to rile the rapidly growing country. As far back as 1820 the Missouri Compromise had banned slavery north of the latitude 36° 30' (with the exception of Missouri itself, which was a slave state). A further, uneasy truce had been reached in 1850 with the passage of a new compromise, a measure engineered by Stephen Douglas, Henry Clay, and Daniel Webster that organized the vast regions west of Iowa and Missouri. Pursuant to the agreement, California was admitted to the Union as a free state, while the territories of New Mexico and Utah, formerly Mexican possessions, would decide for themselves, at later dates, whether slavery would be allowed. The Compromise of 1850 was satisfactory but hardly perfect. "The question of slavery in the territories has been avoided," said Senator Salmon P. Chase of Ohio. "It has not been settled."[9] Despite its faults the compromise did succeed, for a time, in quieting talk of secession and possible hostilities over the slavery issue.

The slavery truce was shattered in 1854, when the Compromise of 1850 was repealed with the passage of the Kansas-Nebraska Act. Proslavery forces, anxious to expand slavery into the million square acres that comprised the territories, found a willing sponsor for the bill in Senator Stephen Douglas, who served as chairman of the powerful Committee on Territories. Douglas's bill divided the territory immediately west of the Missouri River in two: the north would become Nebraska and the south Kansas. Under the concept of "popular sovereignty" the residents of each new territory would determine whether slavery would be legalized there, now and later, when the territories became states. Both Nebraska and Kansas, however, were north of the 36° 30' line; thus the act nullified the provisions of the Missouri Compromise. President Pierce signed the bill into law in May, and Douglas correctly predicted that "a hell of a storm" would ensue.[10]

Douglas took a calculated gamble by engineering passage of the bill. He believed that by removing the slavery question in the territories from Congress and placing it in the hands of those who would live there, a battle between Northern and Southern antagonists could be avoided. But Douglas was horribly mistaken. Democrats and Whigs divided bitterly over the law, with Southerners generally supporting the measure and Northerners opposing. The Whig Party would never recover; it could not even field a presidential candidate in 1856. Abolitionists and Free-Soilers, outraged that slavery might expand, immediately began to pressure Congress to counter the measure. Rather than unite the country, Douglas's law ripped it open along political, sectional, and philosophical lines.

Along with many others, Lincoln was "thunderstruck" and "astounded" when the new law was enacted, for he believed that the Missouri Compromise was a compact of near-sacred importance and had "settled the slavery question forever."[11] Now, he feared, there was a real danger that slavery would spread, perhaps rapidly, and he could no longer stand by. Newly energized and "aroused as never before," he traveled the state and argued against the law, quickly becoming the leader of Illinois's antislavery faction. His political career was suddenly rekindled, as slavery became the central, driving issue of his political concerns.

In Peoria on October 16, 1854, Lincoln gave a speech—his first great speech—that clearly set forth not only his arguments against the Kansas-Nebraska Act but also his personal views on the nature of slavery. He revered the Constitution and acknowledged that it protected slavery; this was nothing more than fidelity to the rule of law. But what Douglas and other proslavery advocates could not and would not understand, charged Lincoln, was that the institution of slavery was morally wrong and a "monstrous injustice" because it denied the "humanity of the negro." The Declaration of Independence (written before the Constitution) had declared that all men were created equal, but now "for *some* men to enslave others is a sacred right of self-government. . . . The spirit of seventy-six, and the spirit of Nebraska, are utter antagonisms; and the former is rapidly being replaced by the latter." Repeal the Missouri Compromise, Lincoln warned, even repeal the Declaration itself, but "you still cannot repeal human nature. It still will be the abundance of man's heart, that slavery extension is wrong." Douglas's assertions about popular sovereignty were illogical and dangerous, Lincoln believed, for slavery was the very antithesis of self-government. "What I do say is, no man is good enough to govern another man, *without that other's consent.* I say this is the leading principle—the sheet anchor of American republicanism."

Lincoln's Peoria speech marked a turning point in his career. Those who heard it, or who read about it in the newspapers, were impressed with its emotional clarity as well as its content. The earnestness with which he spoke, the passionate, serious tone that he took, surprised many who were expecting, perhaps, homespun humor and anecdotes. In his years away from politics he had matured, become galvanized; certainly his views on slavery had evolved. For Lincoln, the passage of the Kansas-Nebraska Act represented a threat to the nation and an assault on the vision of the founding fathers. But it also represented an opportunity for him to move from respected attorney and sometime politician to statesman and prominent national figure.[12]

Lincoln's Peoria speech sparked his emergence onto the national scene through a series of events—successes and failures both—spread over the next six years. He lost in his attempt to claim the Whig nomination for a U.S. Senate seat in 1855, which led to another attack of depression but also deepened his resolve to halt the spread of slavery. And passions on that issue were now running at fever pitch. "Bleeding Kansas" had become a vicious battleground as proslavery and antislavery forces flooded into the territory in hopes of determining the future. Proslavery guerrillas from Missouri sacked the Free-Soil capital of Lawrence, and a religious zealot named John Brown led a group of fanatical abolitionists on a murderous retaliatory rampage. Douglas's cursed law, Lincoln believed, was the cause of all the bloodshed, for it was "conceived in violence, passed in violence, and executed in violence."[13] Lincoln looked to the political party structure to channel his efforts.

But to which party should he belong? He was loyal to the Whigs but had no choice but to accept that the party could not recover from its split over the Kansas-Nebraska Act. "I think I am a Whig," he wrote, "but others say there are no Whigs, and that I am an abolitionist," even though "I do no more than oppose the *extension* of slavery. . . . I am not a Know-Nothing. That is certain. How could I be? How can anyone who abhors the oppression of Negroes be in favor of degrading classes of white people? Our progress in degeneracy appears to me to be pretty rapid. As a nation, we begin by declaring that '*all men are created equal.*' We now practically read it, 'all men are created equal, *except negroes.*' When the Know-Nothings get control, it will read, 'all men are created equal, except negroes, *and foreigners, and catholics.*' "

That left the emerging Republican Party, a coalition of former Whigs, Free-Soilers, and abolitionists, and even antislavery Democrats who wished to band together to fight the Kansas-Nebraska Act and the extension of slavery. (One in four Republicans in the new party was a former Democrat.) By the spring of 1856, Lincoln was ready to join the new party's ranks. "I have no objection to 'fuse' with any body," he said to the Illinois Republican organizer Owen Lovejoy, "providing I can fuse on ground which I think is right."[14] He insisted on a framework for the party that could include all the various factions. The party must oppose the spread of slavery but must also respect the Constitution's protection of slavery where it existed. The party had to avoid "dangerous extremes" (such as pure abolitionists called for) and stake out the middle ground. To attract foreign-born voters, the party must officially advocate religious toleration, and to appease the Know-Nothings it must oppose state funds to parochial schools. Lincoln suggested that the party adopt as its motto the famous words of Daniel Webster: "Liberty and Union, now and forever, one and inseparable." Under these terms and Lincoln's steady leadership, the Illinois Republican Party was launched in May 1856.[15]

Hopeful that the party would meet with eventual success, Lincoln pondered his own political fate. Strangely, his career seemed intertwined with that of Stephen Douglas. He from Kentucky and Douglas from Vermont had settled in the same state, had even courted the same woman, but while Lincoln had almost always met with political disappointment, Douglas had risen like a shooting star. Recalling their first meeting in the state legislature back in 1836, Lincoln wrote, "We were both young then, perhaps he a trifle younger than I. Even then we were both ambitious; I, perhaps, quite as much so as he. With *me*, the race of ambition has been a failure—a flat failure; with *him* it has been one of splendid success."[16] But the game was far from over, and Lincoln sensed that he and Douglas would battle for the Senate in 1858.

While the new president, James Buchanan, hoped that reason and calm would prevail after his victory over the first Republican standard-bearer, John C. Frémont, in the 1856 presidential election, an infamous decision by the U.S. Supreme Court in 1857 ensured that those hopes were naive. In *Dred Scott v. Sandford*, Chief Justice Roger Taney, writing for a divided court, held that a black slave who had been transported to a free state had no standing to sue for his freedom. "Negroes are beings of an inferior order," wrote Taney, ". . . and altogether unfit to associate with the white race . . . they possessed no rights which the white man was bound to respect." Further, wrote Taney in dictum, the Missouri Compromise was unconstitutional insofar as it had outlawed slavery in the territories, for that prohibition violated the property rights clause of the Fifth Amendment.[17] Taney's ruling on the constitutionality of the Missouri Compromise was irrelevant, since that legislation had been invalidated by the Kansas-Nebraska Act, but that ruling was nonetheless significant.

Lincoln condemned the *Dred Scott* decision, for he reasoned that if Congress could not prohibit slavery in the territories the practice would become, in effect, legal everywhere. While the decision was clearly incorrect, Lincoln believed, the ruling was nevertheless binding. It could be negated only by another decision overturning it, and that was something to which Republicans needed to dedicate themselves. Lincoln was doubtless sincere in his view that the high court had the final word on legal issues. But the notion of judicial review of acts of Congress was not then an established view, the precedent of *Marbury v. Madison* notwith-standing. The idea that the court had the absolute and final word on the constitutionality of federal laws still lay decades in the future. Lincoln believed that the Supreme Court ought to be paid deference, and that nothing should be done actively to violate the decision, but he did not believe that the executive had to make a point of enforcing it. Beyond this the president could use his appointive power to change the composition of the court.

While the *Dred Scott* decision was certainly a blow to antislavery sentiment, it seemed also to be a death knell for Stephen Douglas's vision of popular sovereignty, since no territorial legislature could now decide to exclude slavery. His predicament worsened when President Buchanan urged Congress to admit Kansas as a slave state pursuant to a dubious constitutional convention held in Lecompton. Congress deadlocked on the matter, but the resulting split between Douglas and the president (and the Southern Democrats who supported him) would prove decisive.

Lincoln and his supporters saw their opportunity to attack Douglas's vulnerability, and in June 1858 state Republican leaders unanimously passed a resolution endorsing Lincoln as their candidate to oppose Douglas for reelection to the U.S. Senate. On June 16, Lincoln gave his acceptance speech—the second great speech of his career—at the statehouse in Springfield. Using familiar biblical language, and again relying on the Unionist sentiments of Jackson and Webster, Lincoln began his carefully crafted address:

> If we could first know *where* we are, and *whither* we are tending, we could then better judge *what* to do, and *how* to do it.
>
> We are now into the *fifth* year, since a policy was initiated, with the *avowed* object, and *confident* promise, of putting an end to slavery agitation.
>
> Under the operation of that policy, that agitation has not only, *not ceased*, but has *constantly augmented*.

In *my* opinion, it *will* not cease, until a *crisis* shall have been reached, and passed.

"A house divided against itself cannot stand."

I believe this government cannot endure, permanently half *slave* and half *free*.

I do not expect the Union to be *dissolved*—I do not expect the house to *fall*—but I *do* expect it will cease to be divided.[18]

The centerpiece of the campaign, the Lincoln-Douglas debates, became one of the seminal political events in the history of American politics. Thousands of people attended the boisterous affairs, traveling by rail, horse, and wagon. Bands played, parades were organized, and fireworks and cannon fire advertised the pageantry. Newspapers from around the country closely followed the contest between "the Little Giant" and "Honest Abe," for Illinois had become "the most interesting political battleground in the Union."[19] The two men were as much a contrast in styles as in political ideology. Douglas was refined, energetic, and supremely confident. He traveled in high style by private rail car, surrounded by advisers and in the company of his beautiful young wife, Adele. Lincoln was gawky, unkempt, and unassuming. He traveled alone, a forlorn figure with a tattered carpetbag on his lap, lost in silent contemplation.

The debates followed familiar themes. Douglas defended popular sovereignty as the great American and democratic principle, the truest form of self-government. He argued that the government had been founded "on the white basis . . . made by the white man for the benefit of the white man." He attacked Lincoln's "house divided" warnings, arguing that the reckless doctrine was a precursor to civil war. Why couldn't the country endure half slave and half free? he asked. It had so existed for nearly a century. Douglas consistently blasted Lincoln's views that slavery should ultimately become extinct; that meant, he insisted, that Lincoln advocated racial equality. The majority of Americans, Douglas believed, did not support the "amalgamation of the races."[20]

Lincoln was on the defensive in the first debates at Ottawa and Freeport but gained in confidence and hit his stride at Galesburg, Quincy, and Alton. The Democrats would not be satisfied, he charged, until slavery was established in every state. Lincoln did not support full equality for blacks; in fact, he went to great lengths to convince his audiences (particularly those in southern Illinois) that he did not support voting rights for blacks, and did not believe they should sit on juries or hold office. Neither was he in favor of amalgamation; just because he did not want a black woman for a slave, he said, did not necessarily mean that he wanted one for a wife. But he firmly believed, as did the founding fathers, that all Americans, regardless of color, were free to enjoy the fruits of their own labors. Slavery was wrong and would always be wrong, and that was the issue "that will continue in this country when these poor tongues of Judge Douglas and myself shall be silent."[21]

In addition to the seven face-to-face debates, the two candidates appeared separately in cities and towns all across Illinois. Between early July and late October, Lincoln and Douglas traveled almost ten thousand miles and gave two hundred speeches. Ever the political organizer, Lincoln saw to it that the Republican party machine ran at full strength. He raised money, planted articles in state newspapers, and made sure that his speeches were printed in both English and German. But in the end Lincoln's efforts did not pay off. Under the Constitution, U.S. senators were not elected by direct popular vote, but rather were chosen by the state legislatures. In the official balloting in January (following the election of new state representatives in November), Douglas received 54 votes to 46 for Lincoln, and thus was reelected to the Senate.[22]

While Lincoln agonized over yet another defeat, many suggested that he would be a strong contender for the Republican presidential nomination in 1860, and he was flooded with speaking offers from across the country. Finding time whenever his busy court schedule would allow, Lincoln spoke in Wisconsin, Ohio, and Indiana, among other places. He continued to temper his passion with moderation, believing that results must be achieved not through bloodshed but through the ballot box. In Atchison, Kansas, in January 1860 he denounced John Brown's recent attempt to cause a slave revolt at Harper's Ferry, Virginia, warning Southern states that threatened secession that if they left the Union, "it will be our duty to deal with you as old John Brown has been dealt with."

For Lincoln the high-water mark of this period was the speech—his third great speech—that he delivered at New York's Cooper Union in February 1860. Addressing a crowd of fifteen hundred people, including the prominent newspaper editors Horace Greeley and William Cullen Bryant, Lincoln patiently explained his position that the founding fathers had meant for slavery to fade away. Twenty-one of the thirty-nine signers of the Constitution, he pointed out, had at some point supported congressional regulation of slavery in the territories. Republicans like himself sought only to follow the original intentions of the founders, unlike the conspirators Taney, Douglas, and Buchanan, who wanted slavery to spread. Those who spoke of secession were misguided; they followed a "rule or ruin" philosophy. "You say you won't abide the election of a Republican President," he chided. "In that supposed event, you say, you'll destroy the Union and then, you say, the great crime of having destroyed it will be on us." True Republicans must follow the rule of law, hold firm to their principles, to "do nothing through passion and ill temper." And the struggle was surely all about principles. Slavery was an evil that must not be allowed to expand. "Their thinking it is right, and our thinking it wrong, is the precise fact upon which depends the whole controversy. Can we cast their view as our own? Let us not be slandered from our duty by false accusations against us," he thundered as the crowd, now standing, cheered and applauded, "nor frightened from it by menaces of destruction to our government nor of dungeons to ourselves. Let us have faith that right makes might, and in that faith, let us, to the end, dare to do our duty as we understand it."[23]

It is important to understand that while Southerners were wrong in contending that Lincoln was for the amalgamation of the races, they were not wrong in seeing him as a resolute foe of slavery—especially in the vast territories that were not yet states. This was an article of faith with Lincoln.

Lincoln's triumphant address was heralded in the press. He embarked on a speaking tour of the Northeast, appearing before adoring crowds in New Hampshire, Connecticut, and Massachusetts. His political friends back in Illinois, including Norman Judd and Judge David Davis, maneuvered to bring the Republican National Convention to Chicago in May, which gave Lincoln a huge advantage over his party rivals for the nomination. Lincoln's men lobbied hard to persuade delegates to support the moderate Lincoln, who was enough of a newcomer on the national scene that he had few political enemies. Indeed, his rivals all had weaknesses: William Seward of New York was perceived as too radical; Salmon Chase was no certainty to carry his home state of Ohio; Edward Bates of Missouri had once been affiliated with the Know-Nothings; and Pennsylvania's Simon Cameron had a reputation for corruption. Lincoln, who stayed in Springfield for the convention, supposed he was "not the first choice of a very great many," but his managers made deals, promised cabinet posts, and cajoled uncommitted delegates. It was enough for Lincoln to gain the nomination on the second ballot, and Chicago went wild in celebration.[24]

Lincoln and his advisers were smart enough to realize that if no major mistakes were committed, the presidential election would almost certainly be won. The Democratic Party had hopelessly split over the slavery issue, holding two conventions and

nominating two candidates: Douglas, who had the support of
Northern Democrats, and Vice President John C. Breckinridge,
the choice of the Southern Democrats. (A third candidate, John
Bell, had considerable support, especially in the border states and
from former Whigs and Know-Nothings.) Careful not to contradict the popular image of Honest Abe the Rail-splitter, Lincoln
ran on his statements and the platform of the Republican Party.
But many Southerners refused to believe Lincoln's insistence that
he had no inclination, or legal authority, to interfere with slavery
where it existed. If Lincoln were elected, they warned, their way
of life was in jeopardy. Indeed, the galvanizing issue across the
South was that Lincoln was in his soul an enemy of slavery who
would use the power of the White House to put an end to this
way of life. Rather than capitulate to a Republican who wanted
to place blacks on an equal footing with whites, Southern states
threatened to leave the Union. Of course, this was an exaggera-
tion of Lincoln's position. He did not advocate social integration
of the races. But Southerners knew that Lincoln would be an antislavery president. They wanted none of that, even if this meant
their secession from the Union.

Election Day was November 6, and the Republican strategy
worked to perfection. Lincoln was strong in the Northeast and
West. He carried no Southern states, of course; his name was not
even allowed on the ballot in most places there. In the end he tal-
lied 180 electoral votes to 72 for Breckinridge, 39 for Bell, and
only 12 for Douglas. But while those around him celebrated, Lincoln was pensive, for though he held out hope that reason would
prevail in the South, some state legislatures planned immediately
to meet and discuss secession procedures. Lincoln hoped that
these dissatisfied voices would be silenced by patriotism, but he
sensed that troubled times were ahead. "Well, boys, your troubles
are over now," he told a group of journalists who gathered at his
home after the election, "but mine have just begun."[25]

In ten tumultuous years Lincoln's star had risen improbably and remarkably. Only a few years earlier he had been certain that his political career was over, but the exploding issue of slavery gave Lincoln a platform to publicize his evolving, maturing views on the abomination of American society that threatened the very foundation of the republic. Overcoming rejection and defeat, he rose from the ashes of one political party to head another. Firmly believing that the principle of self-government was the essence of freedom, he fused a reverence for the Constitution with an admiring interpretation of the personal liberty that Thomas Jefferson had envisioned in the Declaration of Independence. Utilizing his skills for organization, preparation, and adherence to political principle, Lincoln had been transformed from attorney to candidate to statesman. Fate had brought him to lead the American people in the most calamitous crisis of our national history. No one could know the outcome of the perilous journey that now confronted the newly elected president.

3

Lincoln and the Union

I believe this government cannot endure, permanently half slave and half free. I do not expect the Union to be dissolved . . . but I do expect it will cease to be divided.
> —Abraham Lincoln, Springfield, Illinois, 1858

As he came to the presidency in the winter of 1860–61, Abraham Lincoln was dedicated above all else to preserving a united nation. The cause of Union was, to Lincoln, the cause of freedom and democracy itself. He insisted that no state had the right to disrupt the national authority or to challenge the fundamental concept of majority rule. Lincoln knew he would occupy the office of the president only temporarily and that on his inauguration he would take a solemn oath, "registered in Heaven," to "preserve, protect and defend" the government so that it might be turned over, intact and unharmed, to his successor. Orderly transition, Lincoln knew, reflected the will of the electorate and was the very essence of popular government. He was determined to establish, for all time, that the people's republic could not be reduced to an "absurdity" because of an arbitrary secession of one or more of the states. "We must settle this question now, whether in a free government the minority have the right to break up the government whenever they choose," Lincoln said. "If we fail it will go far to prove the incapability of the people to govern themselves."[1]

No other American president had ever faced the challenges of disunion, rebellion, and civil war. Lincoln met those challenges with firm resolve. Slow to recognize that secession might really occur, he nonetheless took on the role of war president almost from the moment he assumed office. Believing that suppression of rebellion was first and foremost an executive function, Lincoln then took a series of unprecedented actions that may not have been strictly legal in the absence of congressional action or oversight, but were in Lincoln's mind a public necessity. Preservation of the Union was the justification.

Southern states had been threatening secession from the Union for many years. Since the mid-1820s unhappy Southerners had seen a steady erosion of state sovereignty rights, replaced by a stronger, centralized federal government. The South Carolina legislature nullified the Tariff of 1832, with John C. Calhoun taking a more moderate position even though he had laid out the theory of nullification (that is, the idea that states had the right not to be bound by federal laws they disagreed with) four years earlier. South Carolina then served notice that if their nullification was rejected by Washington, they would secede. President Andrew Jackson mobilized federal troops and threatened to use force to uphold the law, and a crisis was averted only when Congress passed compromise legislation. Every election year, it seemed, brought a new chorus of secession threats from the South. Usually the complaint was that some federal action was intruding on matters better left to the states, or that some non-Democratic politician was determined to undermine the Southern way of life. Many believed that the Southern states made a habit of complaining about national legislation as a way of forcing concessions on other matters (passage of the Compromise of 1850, for example, and enforcement of the Fugitive Slave Act), but never once had the South actually carried out its threats. The Republican strategist Carl Schurz sneered that those indignant Southern states would, at most, "secede, go out and take two drinks, and come back again."[2] Many Northern congressmen had grown so tired of decades of empty Southern threats that they did not take seriously the talk of secession that arose in the days surrounding Lincoln's election.

The election of Abraham Lincoln, however, was seen by Southerners as a preemptive act of war. They found many reasons to loathe the man they derided as a "baboon," a "horrid-looking wretch," and a "blood-thirsty tyrant." Lincoln was a "Black Republican" who in their view advocated equality for slaves or, worse, like John Brown, favored insurrection. His proclamation that "a house divided cannot stand" was proof that he wanted war. Lincoln's oft-stated goal of putting slavery on the road to extinction showed that he wanted to cut away the very fabric of Southern life. He would free some four million slaves, which would wreck the Southern economy and replace white workers with black. Southerners suspected that Lincoln would fill patronage positions in the South with political cronies, and soon the region would be filled with antislavery judges, marshals, and postmasters. Inevitably a Southern Republican Party would take root, and any power the slave interests held in Washington would disappear.

Slavery had existed in North America for some 250 years. Southerners had convinced themselves that their slaves were better off financially, spiritually, and socially than they had been in Africa; undoubtedly, they believed, slaves were treated better than poor Northern factory workers, and a "sectional" president representing only Northern interests had no right to change a system that for decades had proven to be peaceful and prosperous. They felt much more than resentment toward Lincoln and the Republicans; an "intense mutual hatred" existed between North and South, said Secretary of the Treasury Howell Cobb, a former governor of Georgia and Speaker of the House, and separation was the only option. On December 20, 1860, just six weeks after Lincoln's election, South Carolina's legislature met and drafted articles of secession. Six more cotton states in the Deep South soon followed, and the Union came apart.[3]

Anxious observers all over the country hoped that President James Buchanan might take steps to resolve the situation diplomatically and peacefully. But the hapless Buchanan proved sorely overmatched by the crisis. He had hoped that the *Dred Scott* decision would settle the slavery question once and for all, but was now dismayed to learn that anger and resentment over the issue had only increased. In his annual message to Congress, delivered on December 3, Buchanan blamed the crisis on the "incessant and violent agitation" of Northern radicals who inspired slaves with "vague notions of freedom." He denied that any state had the right to leave the Union, but then weakly argued that he had no authority to prevent secession. The president was without power to act, he stated; perhaps Congress could devise a remedy. Privately, Buchanan could only hope that civil war would not begin until after he left office on March 4. Meanwhile, a provisional Southern government, headed by luminaries including former senator Jefferson Davis of Mississippi, began to seize federal forts, and federal courthouses and post offices were closed.

Those who looked for Lincoln to speak out on the issue were sorely disappointed. Despite pleas from political friends and enemies alike, and despite relentless questioning by national newspaper reporters, Lincoln chose to remain quiet. He had no power to deal with secession, he believed, until he was inaugurated, and at the very least he could not act until the Electoral College ballots were counted on February 13 and he officially became president-elect. More important, he believed that his views—the same views that had gotten him elected—were well known. "I could say nothing which I have not already said, and which is in print and accessible to the public," he told a reporter.[4] Secessionists would not bluff him into changing his position, even slightly.

"They seek a sign, and no sign shall be given them," he said.[5] Even the urging of Georgian Alexander Stephens (an old friend from Congress and soon to be the Confederate vice president) could not deter him. "A word fitly spoken by you," wrote Stephens, "would indeed be like 'apples of gold in pictures of silver.'"[6] But Lincoln kept his silence.

Despite the militant surge in the South, Lincoln was not fully convinced that the crisis was real. In 1856 he had declared secessionist talk "Humbug, nothing but folly."[7] Now Lincoln remained optimistic that true Unionists (including what he thought was a strong former Whig coalition) outnumbered secessionists in the South and would convince their misguided brethren that it would be foolhardy to follow through with their plan to splinter the Union. He realized that the Gulf states might eventually try to secede, but he hoped that the border states of Virginia, Kentucky, Tennessee, and Missouri would remain loyal. "Let us at all times remember that all American citizens are brothers of a common country," he said, "and should dwell together in the bonds of fraternal feeling."[8] The constitutional order would not be violated, he insisted. Secession was not a question open for debate.

And so Lincoln spent the winter after his election in Springfield, quietly watching events unfold but staying out of sight. He employed two young men, John Hay and John Nicolay, as secretaries, and the loyal pair helped him manage his increasing correspondence and deal with an endless stream of visitors. Many sought political patronage positions, and Lincoln obliged, appointing some twelve hundred men to postmaster, clerk, and customhouse jobs. Lincoln also spent a considerable amount of time selecting his cabinet. Recognizing that his party consisted of differing interest groups, Lincoln tried to strike an unusual balance, selecting men who had been his chief rivals for the Republican nomination, who came from different parts of the country, and who were former Whigs and Democrats. He settled on William Seward of New York as secretary of state; Salmon Chase of Ohio as secretary of the Treasury; Edward Bates of Missouri as attorney general; Montgomery Blair of Maryland as postmaster general; Simon Cameron of Pennsylvania as secretary of war; Caleb Smith of Indiana as secretary of the interior; and Gideon Welles of Connecticut as secretary of the navy. Although this cabinet ultimately produced dividends—Seward, for example, and Edwin Stanton, who would later replace Cameron, became Lincoln's close friends—the group's differences in ideology and personality created difficulties for their president. "No President ever had a Cabinet," said the New York politician Chauncey Depew, "of which the members were so independent, had so large individual followings, and were so inharmonious."[9]

Some historians have argued that Lincoln seriously handicapped his presidency by assembling a cabinet composed of his former rivals, who also had sharply different views with one another. But such top Lincoln scholars as James McPherson and David Donald believed Lincoln had chosen wisely. More recently Doris Kearns Goodwin, in her impressive book *Team of Rivals*, argued that Lincoln as an adroit politician had been wise to pull his opponents into the White House, where by skillful leadership he might find ways to work with them rather than be attacked by them as outside critics. Perhaps this is what a latter-day president, Lyndon Johnson, had in mind when he said, using less decorous language than Lincoln would have employed: "It's better to have a guy in your tent pissing out than to have him outside pissing in."

With armed conflict pending, some members of Congress (including Stephen Douglas) searched for compromise. The better proposals called for reinstating the Missouri Compromise and extending it to the Pacific coast, or for amending the Constitution to forever protect slavery where it existed. Lincoln monitored these attempts but took a hard line against most of them, adamant in his position that slavery must not be extended. If he were to compromise on that issue, he wrote, "all our labor is lost, and, ere long, must be done again. . . . The tug has to come, and better now, than any time thereafter."[10] Lincoln the attorney had always advocated compromise in the legal arena; he knew that negotiation led to settlement, and he believed that litigation should always be the last resort. But to compromise on the extension of slavery would be absurd. He had been legally elected on the premises that slavery would not be extended and that the Union would remain intact. He would not alter those positions now.

In mid-February Lincoln began a two-week train trip to Washington for his inauguration, allowing thousands of people in Indianapolis, Cleveland, Buffalo, New York, and other places to see and hear him for the first time. Looking slightly more distinguished in newly grown whiskers, Lincoln offered little evidence of how he intended to deal with disunion, but stated repeatedly that he intended to enforce the laws and hold on to federal properties. In New Jersey he told an enthusiastic crowd that he would do "all in my power to promote a peaceable settlement of all our difficulties. The man does not live who is more devoted to peace than I am. None who would do more to preserve it. But it may be necessary to put the foot down firmly. And if I do my duty, and do right, you will sustain me, will you not?"[11] The next day newspapers across the country quoted this, Lincoln's first declaration that force might be required to hold the Union together. Fearful of a rumored assassination attempt in Baltimore, Lincoln switched trains and stole into Washington before dawn, a decision that proved embarrassing and one he would regret.

Finally, Inauguration Day came on March 4, 1861. Lincoln's address to the nation was the most anticipated in American history, and he had spent weeks in preparing it, showing drafts only to Orville Browning, a Republican senator from Illinois and a friend and critic of Lincoln's, and William Seward. The speech was his best chance, and his first as president, to set forth his views on the Union, the Constitution, and the integrity of the United States. He saw no reason to speak of issues *other* than secession and the Union, he told the crowd of thirty thousand people assembled at the East Portico of the Capitol; no other issues caused "special anxiety, or excitement."[12] He sought first to assure apprehensive Southerners, in plain and simple language, that "their property, and their peace, and personal security" were in no danger. His administration would protect their slave system and enforce fugitive slave laws as mandated by the Constitution. He had always said, and now said again, "I have no purpose, directly or indirectly, to interfere with the institution of slavery in the States where it exists. I believe I have no lawful right to do so, and I have no inclination to do so."

But despite his repeated assurances, Lincoln continued, "a disruption of the Federal Union heretofore only menaced, is now formidably attempted." That, he stated, could never be allowed to happen. "I hold, that in contemplation of universal law, and of the Constitution, the Union of these States is perpetual. Perpetuity is implied, if not expressed, in the fundamental law of all national governments. It is safe to assert that no government proper, ever had a provision in its organic law for its own termination." That the Union was perpetual was confirmed by its own history, Lincoln stated. It was "formed" by the 1774 Articles of Association; "matured" by the 1776 Declaration of Independence; and "further matured" and endorsed by the thirteen colonies in 1778. Finally, the founding fathers had "ordained and enacted" the Constitution with the words *"In order to form a more perfect Union."* Destruction of the Union could only mean that "the Union is *less* perfect than before the Constitution, having lost the vital element of perpetuity." The actions of any state to leave the Union of its own accord, he said, were "legally void." The Union, then, remained "unbroken."[13]

As president, Lincoln was obligated to enforce the laws in all the states. He would see to it, he said, to hold and occupy federal posts, collect duties, and deliver the mail. In performing these simple tasks, he promised, "There will be no bloodshed or violence . . . unless it be forced upon the national authority." Again he sought to soothe the fears of Southerners: "there will be no invasion—no using of force against, or among the people anywhere." In every situation, he promised, even in those involving "obnoxious strangers" who sought to interfere with federal functions, Lincoln would use his "best discretion" to resolve the matter peacefully.[14]

Those angry Southerners who were bent on disunion and destruction would not listen to his words, Lincoln knew. But he also knew that there were many others who felt differently. To those, "who really love the Union," he asked, "may I not speak?"[15]

Think clearly and deliberately before you act, he told them. Nothing would be gained, yet much would be lost, by moving recklessly to "destroy our national fabric." Would you "hazard so desperate a step" when the "ills you fly from . . . have no real existence? Will you risk the commission of so fearful a mistake?" Has any right "so plainly written in the Constitution" been denied? "I think not," he said.[16] The rights of the minority would always be protected by the majority, which was held safely in restraint by constitutional checks and balances; that was how the national government endured. For the minority to break from the Union—to secede—simply because it found itself in the minority was, Lincoln said, the "the essence of anarchy."[17]

The only substantial dispute between North and South, Lincoln asserted, was slavery. "One section of our country believes slavery is *right*, and ought to be extended, while the other believes slavery is *wrong*, and ought not to be extended." The Fugitive Slave Law and the suppression of the foreign slave trade now struck an imperfect balance, which might only be made worse after separation of the two sections. Physically speaking, said Lincoln, "we cannot separate. We cannot remove our respective sections from each other, nor build an impassable wall between them. . . . Suppose you go to war, you cannot fight always; and when, after much loss on both sides, and no gain on either, you cease fighting, the identical old questions . . . are again upon you."[18] All the authority of the president, he continued, comes from the people, "and they have conferred none upon him to fix terms for the separation of the States." The people themselves can do this if they choose, but the executive, as such, has nothing to do with it. His duty is to administer the present government and "to transmit it, unimpaired by him, to his successor." Since the power ultimately rests with the people, if they wish they can turn elected officials out of office "at very short intervals." No administration, and certainly not his, said Lincoln, "by any extreme wickedness or folly, can very seriously injure the government, in the short space of four years."

And just as the power to elect and dismiss presidents came from the people, so too did the power to decide the direction of the country. "In *your* hands, my dissatisfied countrymen, and not in mine, is the momentous issue of civil war. The government will not assail *you*. You have no conflict, without being yourselves the aggressors. *You* have no oath registered in Heaven to destroy the government, while *I* shall have the most solemn one to 'preserve, protect, and defend' it."[19]

Lincoln had delivered the bulk of his message clearly, logically, and, he hoped, persuasively, like a lawyer setting out his case for the jury. Even his remarks regarding slavery had lacked the emotional content of recent speeches. Now, still speaking to those who harbored disunion, he closed poetically, his words reflecting Seward's suggestions but uniquely, beautifully, his own. "I am loth to close," he said. "We are not enemies, but friends. We must not be enemies. Though passion may have strained, it must not break our bonds of affection. The mystic chords of memory, stretching from every battle-field, and patriot grave, to every living heart and hearthstone, all over this broad land, will yet swell the chorus of the Union, when again touched, as surely they will be, by the better angels of our nature."[20]

Lincoln's pleas for caution went unheeded in the South. In the weeks after the inauguration, secessionists took control of still more federal forts, transferred monies from the U.S. Mint in New Orleans to the new government of what was called the Confederate States of America, and boldly seized the USS *Isabella*. Eventually only two federal installations in the South, Fort Pickens off the coast of Florida and Fort Sumter in Charleston Bay, South Carolina, remained under federal control. While Pickens seemed safely out of reach of Confederate cannon, the eyes of the world were on Sumter. Its commanding officer had advised Lincoln that the fort was in immediate danger of falling into rebel hands, and reinforcements were urgently needed. Lincoln's administration watched events unfold and struggled to come up with a policy. Lincoln listened to the advice of his cabinet, conferred with state governors and his military leaders (most importantly General Winfield Scott, the hero of the Mexican War and now the head of the Army of the Potomac), and pondered his options.

He was becoming more and more certain that war was inevitable. But if and when conflict came, it would not be the result of Lincoln or his policies. He had to appease moderate Northerners without losing the support of the militants. He also believed it crucial to keep the border states of Delaware, Maryland, Kentucky, and Missouri within the Union fold. Lincoln had promised the nation that he would not be the aggressor, but Sumter was still under federal control and that control needed to be maintained. On April 6 Lincoln sent a letter to the governor of Virginia notifying him of his intent to supply Sumter with provisions only, and not soldiers or armaments. This move in effect forced the hand of the South Carolina rebels, who predictably saw Lincoln's move as an act of aggression and fired on Sumter on April 12. Both sides incorrectly predicted a short war. What came instead was four years of hell.

∙   ∙   ∙

Lincoln was absolutely committed to preserving the Union and constitutional order. He could not bring himself to refer to the actions of the South as "secession," because he did not believe secession existed as a possibility under the Constitution. Rather, it was "rebellion" against the government. Lincoln never recognized the Confederate States of America as a sovereign nation. He never acknowledged the legitimacy of the Confederate government, refusing to negotiate with its ambassadors or representatives. With this mind-set he took a series of unprecedented steps over the course of the war, stripping away some of the protections guaranteed by the Constitution, and all in the name of preserving the Union.

Lincoln's setting aside the protection of habeas corpus and his other extralegal actions, including the censorship of newspapers critical of his administration, are doubtless understandable. But serious questions as to their legality are justified. It is also debatable whether these actions enhanced the power of the Union or shortened the war. Breaking the law is ordinarily not a good idea, even in wartime.

Habeas corpus, often referred to as a centerpiece of American liberty, is the judicial mandate ordering prison officials to bring an inmate before the court so the legality of the arrest can be determined. Article I, section 9, of the U.S. Constitution states: "The writ of the privilege of habeas corpus shall not be suspended, unless when in cases of rebellion or invasion, the public safety may require it." Lincoln was fearful that Maryland, a slave state, would secede or, at the very least, disrupt communications between Washington and other government outposts in the North. He also was concerned that rebel forces might attack the capital and overrun it before sufficient forces could arrive and defend it; therefore military routes to Washington had to be held open. Thus Lincoln believed that the "extremest necessity" existed, and on April 27 he ordered that habeas corpus be suspended "at any point on or in the vicinity of the military line . . . between the City of Philadelphia and the City of Washington." The line would later that year be extended all the way to Maine, and in 1863 the writ was suspended throughout the United States. Although records were poorly kept, best estimates indicate that more than thirteen thousand citizens were arrested over the course of the war without benefit of habeas corpus, most of whom were Southerners and had committed (or were suspected of) desertion, spying, supplying aid to the enemy, intimidating Unionists, or other offenses.[21] Those arrested were tried in military, not civilian, courts.

General Winfield Scott quickly arrested Baltimore's mayor and police marshal, the chief clerk of the Maryland Senate, and nine members of the Maryland state legislature. Amid mounting criticism from Democrats who accused Lincoln of tyranny, Chief Justice Taney (sitting on a federal district court) ruled that only Congress, and not the president, had the power to suspend the writ.[22] Lincoln's administration ignored Taney's order. Instead, in his message to Congress on July 4, Lincoln asked whether "all the law, *but one*, [were] to go unexecuted, and the government itself to go to pieces, lest that one be violated?" Congress had not been in session when exigent circumstances dictated that habeas corpus be suspended, he argued. A day later, Attorney General Edward Bates opined that the three branches of the federal government were "co-ordinate and coequal" and that, in constitutional matters, the judgment of one was not binding upon another. Thus was Taney's roadblock set aside.

In March 1863 the Republican Congress passed the Habeas Corpus Indemnity Act, which justified Lincoln's actions and afforded him the power to suspend habeas corpus throughout the United States. The law required the War Department to furnish a list of prisoners to federal courts within thirty days of arrest. Lincoln's unprecedented suspension of habeas corpus had been criticized, but he believed that events of rebellion justified and vindicated him. Secretary of the Navy Gideon Welles agreed. "Few, comparatively, know or can appreciate the actual condition of things and state of feelings of the Administration in those days," he later wrote. "Congress had adjourned without making any provision for the storm, though aware it was at hand and soon to burst upon the country. A new administration, scarcely acquainted with each other, and differing essentially in the past, was compelled to act, promptly and decisively."[23]

Lincoln took other extraordinary measures without congressional approval to aid the war effort. He ordered a blockade of Southern ports and expended funds for the purchase and production of weapons. Recognizing that newspapers were political institutions, he did not hesitate to encourage government censorship and control of certain publications. He saw to it that military news originating from Washington was censored, and he regulated telegraph news through the War Department. Occasionally newspaper editors were arrested. Most notably, in 1864 Lincoln ordered the arrest of the editors and publishers of the New York *World* and New York *Journal of Commerce*, Democratic papers that had published a bogus presidential proclamation calling for the draft of four hundred thousand soldiers. In 1863 he approved, for a short time, the suppression of the Chicago *Times* for "disloyal and incendiary sentiments" after that paper had criticized emancipation. For the most part, however, Lincoln was wary of measures that suppressed free speech. He believed that those serious steps should only be taken when editors and publishers were causing "palpable injury to the Military," and he ordered his generals to proceed with "great caution, calmness and forbearance" when investigating questionable activity.

Lincoln utilized the suspension of habeas corpus to enforce military conscription. Initially he called for a massive volunteer force—three hundred thousand men—to fight for the Union, but the results were disappointing. Under the Militia Act of 1862 the president was authorized to issue rules to apply to those states that failed to meet their volunteer quotas. Lincoln interpreted this to mean that he could order a draft, and he did so immediately, becoming the first president to authorize conscription. A year later Congress passed legislation that provided for exemptions and substitutions for those who wished to avoid service and could pay a fee for someone else to take their place. Critics charged that the draft was unconstitutional and a violation of civil liberties. Some states, including New Jersey and New York, asked that they be exempted from the draft, and in July 1863 rioting Irish Americans terrorized New York City, killing more than one hundred people. But Lincoln was resolute, and the draft continued; over the course of the war nearly 164,000 men were drafted or served as substitutes. Under Lincoln's direction, Secretary of War Stanton ordered that draft-eligible citizens could not travel to foreign countries; those who tried to do so were subject to arrest and mandatory military duty and had no right to petition for habeas corpus.

Amid mounting criticism, and the actions of a few judges who granted writs of habeas corpus discharging draftees, Lincoln reacted defensively. Complaints about the draft were "false arguments," he said, coming from those who wanted to find a way out of "disagreeable things." Congress had the explicit authority to raise an army and had acted legally and appropriately in granting him the power to enforce fair rules to make the draft work. Privately Lincoln questioned the patriotism of those who resisted the draft. He thought that "every patriot should willingly take his chance under a law made with great care in order to secure fairness." He also defended the $300 substitution fee as a moderate one, and to those who complained about the price he wondered, "Are we degenerate? Has the manhood of our race run out?"[24]

Lincoln further stretched the limits of presidential authority when he issued the Emancipation Proclamation on January 1, 1863. He had no specific constitutional authority to do so; more precisely, perhaps, he had no authority to confiscate personal property without providing compensation. But the proclamation was a war measure taken by the commander in chief, meant to weaken the enemy. Confederate states were in "actual armed rebellion against the authority and government of the United States," and the measure was "a fit and necessary war measure" for suppressing that rebellion; Lincoln claimed the authority to free slaves only in those rebel states. Still, as with nearly everything he did, Lincoln faced criticism for his proclamation. He defended his action in a letter that was read aloud at a rally in Springfield in September 1863:

> You dislike the emancipation proclamation; and, perhaps, would have it retracted. You say it is unconstitutional—I think differently. I think the constitution invests its Commander-in-chief, with the law of war, in time of war. The most that can be said, if so much, is, that slaves are property. Is there—has there ever been—any question that by the law of war, property, both of enemies and friends, may be taken when needed? And is it not needed whenever taking it, helps us, or hurts the enemy? Armies, the world over, destroy enemy's property when they can not use it; and even destroy their own to keep it from the enemy.

Lincoln never wavered in his devotion to save the Union. Every action he took was calculated to achieve that end. He did not act to gain personal renown; he did not stretch the limits of presidential power because he was interested in power per se. If he favored a liberal interpretation of the Constitution it was because he wanted to save the Constitution, and the country, from the chaos of secession. The sacred document so carefully crafted by the framers bestowed upon the executive great powers, to be used judiciously, in times of great crisis. This Lincoln understood better than anyone else.

4

Lincoln and Emancipation

Fellow citizens, we cannot escape history. . . . In giving free-dom to the slave, we assure freedom to the free. . . . We shall nobly save or meanly lose the last best hope of earth.

—Abraham Lincoln, Second Annual Message to Congress, 1862

On March 5, 1860, eight months before his election and one year before his inauguration, Abraham Lincoln gave a speech in Hartford, Connecticut. "The slave question," he said, "is the prevailing question before the nation. Though it may be true, and probably is true, that all parties, factions and individuals desire it should be settled, it still goes on unsettled—the all-prevailing and all-pervading question of the day."[1] Lincoln would take on the issue three years later, on his own terms, when he utilized the war powers of the executive office and issued the Emancipation Proclamation. The rebellion provided an avenue for Lincoln to transform himself from a president to a constitutional commander in chief. More significantly, the proclamation transformed the meaning of the war itself and redefined for all time the notion of freedom in America. Necessarily limited in scope, the proclamation was both praised and criticized when it was issued; it is often misunderstood and remains a source of debate and analysis today. Lincoln's order freed four million slaves with the stroke of a pen. It was more than just his greatest accomplishment. It was, he believed, "the great event of the nineteenth century."[2]

At the outset of the war Lincoln had made it clear, as did the Republican platform of 1860, that he would not take action against slavery in the Southern states where it existed, but would not permit its extension into the territories. He left no doubt about his opposition to the secession of any state, nor was there any question about his dedication to preserving the Union. But he underestimated the anger his election brought to many Southerners. They believed that he meant to end their slave system and destroy their traditional way of life. Lincoln clung to the belief that loyal Unionists in the South would calm the fears of dissenters, and that talk of secession would wane. When it became obvious that those hopes were futile and that war would ensue, Lincoln waited for his chance to "strike hard" at the institution that he hated so deeply and fulfill the promise he made as a young man.

Just as success for the North in the war effort was a long time in coming, so too was Lincoln's move to end slavery. His views on slavery had evolved over the years, cautiously, prudently. He approached the issue with the reasoning of a lawyer, carefully considering the widely divergent positions of citizens from around the country. At the opposite poles were proponents who wanted slavery to thrive and spread and abolitionists who wanted the practice eradicated immediately. In between were the moderates of varying kinds including antislavery Unionists like Lincoln and Unionist slaveholders in the upper South who opposed secession but wanted to keep their slaves. Others of less defined views simply hoped that common ground could be found and bloodshed avoided. Ever the pragmatist, Lincoln sought to balance his personal animosity toward the "peculiar institution" with his intellectual interpretation of the Constitution, which told him that the federal government could not eradicate slavery in states where it already existed.

Lincoln's approach to the issue started with his personal view, often expressed privately and sometimes publicly, that he abhorred slavery. Though he was born in Kentucky, a slave state (more than one thousand slaves resided in Harlan County alone, and an uncle and great-uncle owned slaves), Lincoln's parents belonged to an antislavery Baptist church. He believed that the family had left Kentucky, at least in part, to get away from slavery, and he described himself as naturally antislavery. In fact, he "could not remember when he did not so think, and feel."[3] As a young man of twenty-one he had witnessed, for the first time, the brutal realities of the sale of slaves while on a riverboat trip down the Mississippi. He had first publicly proclaimed his opposition to slavery in the Illinois legislature in 1837, calling the institution "an injustice and founded on bad policy."[4] While in Congress he had supported the Wilmot Proviso, which outlawed slavery in new territories acquired from Mexico, and he tried to abolish slavery in the District of Columbia. He was never an abolitionist, because he firmly believed that slavery was constitutionally protected in states where it already existed. He nonetheless declared forcefully, "I have always hated slavery, I think as much as any Abolitionist."[5]

Unlike the abolitionists, however, Lincoln was not preoccupied with slavery in his early or middle adult years, perhaps because it did not affect him personally, and perhaps because he was confident that the nation was slowly moving toward freedom for all. Robert H. Brown, a resident of Bloomington, Illinois, heard Lincoln say in a speech in 1854: "The slavery question often bothered me as far back as 1836–40. I was troubled and grieved over it; but after the annexation of Texas I gave it up, believing as I now do, that God will settle it, and settle it right, and that he will, in some inscrutable way, restrict the spread of so great an evil; but for the present it is our duty to wait."[6]

It was the Kansas-Nebraska Act of 1854, which repealed the

Compromise of 1850, fueled by the *Dred Scott* decision in 1857, that pulled Lincoln back into politics. These events quickened his concern with slavery. He reemerged on the political scene, injecting, for the first time, a moral argument into the debate. In typical fashion he studied the history of slavery in the Americas, growing so confident in the subject that he believed he knew more about it than those who criticized his positions. "Slavery is founded in the selfishness of man's nature—opposition to it in his love of justice," he said in his Peoria speech in 1854.[7] Slavery violated the promise of the Declaration of Independence, he argued over and over again, because it negated liberty and equality. In denying the slave the right to enjoy the fruits of his own labor, Lincoln believed, slavery denied him the basic freedom to "make himself," to improve his station in life—as he himself had done. African Americans, Lincoln believed, were human beings and by "natural law" deserved to be treated with dignity and respect. When Stephen Douglas asserted, during the 1858 debates, that the founding fathers did not mean to include blacks in their assertion that "all men are created equal," Lincoln sharpened his argument against Douglas's position. As early as 1854 Lincoln had seen slavery as "a monstrous evil." But with Douglas facing him, he described slavery as "the eternal struggle between right and wrong—throughout the world."[8]

His position on slavery notwithstanding, Lincoln nonetheless shared the commonplace racial prejudices of white society in the nineteenth century. He did not believe that blacks were necessarily the equal of whites on social levels. He did not approve of interracial marriage and did not advocate black suffrage. Like many people, he was not at all sure that blacks and whites could ever live together in harmony in America. "Though Mr. Lincoln shared the prejudices of his white fellow countrymen against the Negro," said Frederick Douglass, "it is hardly necessary to say that in his heart of hearts he loathed and hated slavery."[9] The historian Don E. Fehrenbacher wrote, "It is a mistake to assume that Lincoln's actions in relation to the Negro were determined or even strongly influenced by his racial outlook. He based his antislavery philosophy squarely upon perception of the slave as a person, not as a Negro. According to the Declaration of Independence, he said, all men, including black men, are created equal, at least to the extent that none has a right to enslave another."[10]

Lincoln the humanist scoffed at those who defended slavery on the grounds that blacks were better off as slaves in America than as "heathens" in Africa or as factory workers in the North. "Although volume upon volume is written to prove slavery a very good thing," he said, "we never hear of the man who wishes to take the good of it, *by being a slave himself*."[11] In an 1859 letter to Congressman Henry Pierce of Massachusetts, he took the argument further. "Those who deny freedom to others, deserve it not for themselves, and, under a just God, can not long retain it."[12] Slavery was "wrong, morally and politically," and Lincoln could even frame his view of democracy around the issue: "So I would not be a slave, so I would not be a master."

For all his moralizing, Lincoln looked for a political escape from the issue. Like his hero Henry Clay, he had long backed the idea of colonization, or "voluntary emigration" of free blacks to Africa, the West Indies, or elsewhere away from the American mainland. The American Colonization Society began settlement of blacks in Liberia in 1820, but the cost and other difficulties beset the effort from the beginning. During the first years of his presidency Lincoln continued to back colonization, perhaps in an attempt to mollify Northerners who feared a great influx of blacks (and black workers) after emancipation. Although some federal money was made available through the Second Confiscation Act, attempts to move blacks to Colombia and Haiti proved fruitless, and by 1864 Lincoln seems to have abandoned the idea entirely.

His cabinet, never a close group, was as deeply divided over the slavery issue as was the rest of the nation. The discussion over the issue and what direction the president should take became marked by bitter and rancorous debate. Personal relationships were severely strained, and the professional interaction among members fell off dramatically; things got so bad that by the summer of 1862 the group stopped meeting regularly. Finally, at Lincoln's direction, the cabinet began to meet every Tuesday and Friday (although the men stubbornly remained in their offices until summoned by a secretary). At these meetings each cabinet member spoke freely and frankly, expressing his views on the slavery question. Lincoln listened but generally remained silent on the subject. His plan to take the historic step of emancipation was percolating in his mind.[13]

Slavery presented a less abstract but still delicate problem in the border states of Delaware, Maryland, Kentucky, and Missouri. All were slave states but did not join the Confederacy, and Lincoln could not afford to alienate them with a new policy of emancipation. Just as he had endorsed a plan of compensated emancipation in the District of Columbia while he was in Congress, Lincoln sought to negotiate a similar plan in the border states, calculating the price for each slave at $400. Lincoln had high hopes for his proposal; his "whole soul was absorbed in it," remembered his old friend David Davis. In early 1862 Lincoln invited state representatives to the White House to discuss his plan, arguing that compensated emancipation would work to shorten the war. Though the leaders balked at his proposal, Lincoln persisted. Later that summer, even while he was seriously contemplating the issuance of the Emancipation Proclamation, Lincoln held a second meeting with border state leaders. "The incidents of the war cannot be avoided," he warned them. "If the war continues long, as it must, if the object be not sooner attained, the institution in your states will be extinguished by mere friction and abrasion—by the mere incidents of war. It will be gone, and you will have nothing valuable in lieu of it."[14]

But the border states would have none of this, and in the wake of this rejection Lincoln had to determine if he should take another route. He spent more time in careful reflection. He "dwelt earnestly on the gravity, importance, and delicacy" of the subject, he told Gideon Welles. And he came to the conclusion that the powers of the office he held, and the circumstances of the rebellion, allowed him to free slaves in the South. He decided to issue the Emancipation Proclamation.

The doctrine of military necessity justified Lincoln's action. Congress was limited in its powers to deal with slavery, he knew. But the war gave the president authority that he never would have had in times of peace. Lincoln came to believe that in cases of armed rebellion against the government, his powers as commander in chief had to be commensurate with those of any ruler whose country had been invaded. Emancipation was a "military necessity absolutely essential for the salvation of the Union," he said. "[We must] free the slaves or be ourselves subdued."[15] In this situation, the constitutional war powers of the president worked to override the constitutional protection for slavery.[16]

Pursuant to the Constitution, slaves were, of course, property, and Lincoln recognized that "under the law of war, property, both of friends or enemies, may be taken when needed."[17] While the legality of this "taking" was debatable, there had been one instance of a similar action in American military history. During the Seminole Wars in the Florida swamps in the 1830s, the guerrilla tactics of the Indians proved to be highly effective against the U.S. Army. When some Indians and their slaves were captured, General Zachary Taylor deported both slaves and masters to the Indian Territory of Oklahoma. Significantly, the U.S. government did not recognize hostile Indian tribes as foreign nations; rather, they were insurgents or rebels against federal authority, just as the Confederates were in 1862.

Looking to Europe, Lincoln saw that the practice of emancipating and arming an enemy's slaves had been recognized as an acceptable means of warfare for nearly two centuries. It was so regarded because slaves and slave labor were used extensively in the war effort. Lincoln knew that slave labor was an essential component of the Confederate army. The rebel government had, in fact, forced slaves into service as laborers, cooks, musicians, teamsters, and other support roles even before it drafted white men into the army. They provided much of the logistical "tail" of the army (functions initially performed by white soldiers and civilians in the federal forces) and thereby freed a higher proportion of the Confederate soldiers for combat duty. Lincoln understood that any maneuver, including emancipation, that might hurt the enemy's chances of success was a legitimate military action.

And Lincoln knew that freedom would also provide the slaves themselves with an incentive to fight for the Union. Slaves had to act boldly in running from their masters and finding their way to Union lines, but Lincoln was confident they would be willing to take the risk if freedom was the reward. "Negroes, like other people, act upon motives," he wrote. "Why should they do anything for us if we will do nothing for them? If they stake their lives for us, they must be prompted by the strongest motive, even the promise of freedom. And the promise, being made, must be kept."[18]

Satisfied that military necessity justified emancipation, Lincoln had to inform his cabinet. He first read a draft of his proclamation to the group in July 1862. Though Lincoln's mind was made up, he valued the opinions of his advisers and encouraged their comments. Salmon Chase and Montgomery Blair thought that emancipation would exceed the scope of presidential power. Furthermore, it would hurt the Republicans in the upcoming congressional elections and might drive the border states into the Confederacy. Surprisingly, Edward Bates, one of the most conservative men in the government, endorsed Lincoln's plan. One of Bates's sons was fighting for the rebels, while four others served the Union. If emancipation would bring a quick end to the conflict, he reasoned, the brothers would never have to face each other on the battlefield. Send the newly freed blacks to Central

America, advised Bates, and be done with the issue once and for all. Gideon Welles and Caleb Smith offered no opinion and no advice.

Secretary of State William Seward provided a thoughtful, intricate analysis. He believed that emancipation would trigger a panic among European nations; some of those nations, fearful that servile unrest in the South would produce anarchy in the cotton markets, might come to the aid of the Confederacy. This must not be allowed to happen, he warned. He did not share Lincoln's confidence that the vast majority of Europeans wished for the eradication of slavery and would not allow economic interests to dissuade them from support of the proclamation. Seward was also concerned about public support for emancipation in America itself. Unionists in the North were hungry for good news from the battlefield. Seward understood that Lincoln was determined to free the slaves; now he had to decide on the proper time to issue his proclamation. He insisted that *when* emancipation would occur was just as important as *how* and *why* it should occur. At the very least, Seward believed, Lincoln must delay his action until a Union victory, lest it appear that the move was merely "the last measure of an exhausted government." Once the "eagle of victory takes his flight," Seward suggested, Lincoln could "hang [the] proclamation about his neck."[19]

Lincoln took this advice to heart. "The wisdom of the view of the Secretary of State struck me with very great force," he said later. "It was an aspect of the case that, in all my thought upon the subject, I had entirely overlooked."[20] The proclamation, he realized, had to be issued from the perspective of power and success, not of defeat. He would wait for a Union victory.

· · ·

Lincoln filed the draft proclamation in a drawer in his office at the White House, then bided his time and used the press to publicize his views on slavery and the Union. Horace Greeley, the editor of the New York *Tribune*, had written an editorial entitled "The Prayer of Twenty Millions," criticizing Lincoln's administration as lacking resolve and insisting that the slaves be freed as a way to weaken the Confederacy. Lincoln wrote a reply on August 22, knowing that it would be published in the paper that boasted the largest circulation in the country, and he used this platform to justify his positions and pave the way for the proclamation that he knew was coming. In effect, Lincoln sought to soften the blow of emancipation for skeptical Northerners. "My paramount object in this struggle is to save the Union, and is *not* either to save or destroy slavery," Lincoln wrote. "If I could save the Union without freeing *any* slave I would do it, and if I could save it by freeing *all* the slaves I would do it; and if I could save it by freeing some and leaving others alone I would also do that. What I do about slavery and the colored race, I do because I believe it helps to save the Union; and what I forbear, I forbear because I do *not* believe it would help save the Union."[21] His carefully worded letter showed a cunning lawyer and a master politician at work. By stressing the Union as his primary concern, Lincoln hoped to make emancipation more palatable for those opposing it.

One month later, Lincoln received word of the victory he had been waiting for. When General George McClellan turned back Robert E. Lee's Maryland invasion at Antietam, Lincoln decided the time had come. On September 22 he announced a preliminary emancipation that in effect gave rebel states one hundred days to return to the Union. If they did not, slaves in those states would be declared forever free. By Christmas it was clear that the Confederates had no intention of repenting, and on January 1, 1863, Lincoln issued the Emancipation Proclamation.

It was written in dry, dispassionate language that lacked the moral tone of his best-known speeches and any emotional outrage at the barbarity of slavery. In fact, there was no indication of Lincoln's personal animosity toward the institution. Instead, the document relied upon his role as commander in chief and set forth its primary purpose of keeping the Union intact, and not of freeing people held in bondage:

> Now, therefore I, Abraham Lincoln, President of the United States, by virtue of the power in me vested as Commander-in-Chief, of the Army and Navy of the United States in time of actual armed rebellion against the authority and government of the United States, and as a fit and necessary war measure for suppressing said rebellion, do, on this first day of January, in the year of our Lord one thousand eight hundred and sixty-three . . . order and declare that all persons held as slaves within said designated States, and parts of States, are, and henceforward shall be free.

Immediately the proclamation was met with criticism and skepticism. Southern slave owners, of course, ignored Lincoln's order, since they did not consider themselves, or their states, part of the Union and did not recognize Lincoln as their president. Radicals and abolitionists believed the measure fell far short of what it might have been. They noted the obvious irony: Lincoln had not freed a single slave in the North (the areas he controlled) and had freed slaves in the South (where he had no control whatsoever). His proclamation, they protested, was a hollow, meaningless stunt. Some questioned the legality of the proclamation on constitutional grounds. Lincoln and the Republicans had always argued that slavery was federally protected, they said. Certainly he had far exceeded his presidential powers in issuing the order.

The proclamation was met with indignant anger in the South. Lincoln was a fiend, a devil whose sole purpose was to spark servile insurrection. Democrats scoffed at Lincoln's hypocrisy; he had, after all, repeatedly promised that he would not touch the institution of slavery. The proclamation showed his true colors, they smugly noted, and Southern acts of secession were now clearly justified. The proclamation was the "most startling political crime . . . yet known in American history," shouted the newspapers in Richmond, Virginia, the capital of the Confederacy. With "a dash of the pen" it had "destroyed four thousand millions of our property." The Confederate president, Jefferson Davis, predicted that reunification of the United States had been rendered forever impossible, and the "entire newspaper press of the Confederacy," said one editor, "echoed the sentiment of the President."[22]

Conservatives worried that Lincoln had gone too far and would alienate voters in the North, who had elected Lincoln on the premise that he would prosecute the war in order to preserve the Union and not to free slaves. (In at least one regard they were correct: in the midterm elections Republicans would lose forty-five seats in the House of Representatives.) Many doubted that Union troops would willingly fight to support emancipated blacks, much less serve alongside them.

For the most part the criticisms were unfounded. Despite its expansive wording, the proclamation was necessarily limited. Because Lincoln acted out of his war power authority, it applied only to states "in armed rebellion" against the government, or those that had seceded from the Union. The four slave states that had not joined the Confederacy (Delaware, Maryland, Kentucky, and Missouri) were not in rebellion, and Lincoln's war powers had no reach over them. The proclamation also exempted those parts of the Confederacy that had already come under federal control, including parts of Louisiana and Virginia. Was freeing the slaves in the Confederacy nothing more than symbolic, since the proclamation was ignored? Many historians answer the question this way: Did the Declaration of Independence really make America independent, since Britain still claimed ownership of the colonies?

The historian Richard Striner has it right: "Lincoln was a rare man, indeed: a fervent idealist endowed with a remarkable gift for strategy. An ethicist, Lincoln was also an artist in the Machiavellian use of power. It was a combination of qualities that made Lincoln's contribution to the antislavery movement so demonstrably necessary."[23] Lincoln was nothing less than a relentless foe of slavery biding his time to strike it at the most opportune and promising moment.

As for the legality of the proclamation, Lincoln knew that too much was at stake to worry about strict constitutional interpretations. The war was a severe national emergency, and it justified actions that might normally not be implemented or even considered. "I felt that measures, otherwise unconstitutional, might become lawful," Lincoln said, "by becoming indispensable to the preservation of the Constitution, through the preservation of the nation."[24] Most significantly, Lincoln recognized that his proclamation had to be followed quickly by a constitutional amendment abolishing slavery. He lobbied hard for such a measure, and his efforts were successful. The Thirteenth Amendment was ratified in 1865, sealing the work the proclamation had begun, and before any legal challenges to it could be made. Legal arguments as to the legitimacy of his order became moot.

While the Emancipation Proclamation did not practically or immediately free a single slave, it was truly a revolutionary document, for it fundamentally and dramatically transformed the character of the war. Now there was added a moral, humanitarian force to the Union cause, and the humanitarian struggle to expand the domain of freedom would transcend the original war effort to preserve the Union. From the date of its issuance, every advance of federal troops, every victory in the field, furthered Lincoln's goal of dignity for all of America's citizens. "Great is the virtue of this Proclamation," wrote Ralph Waldo Emerson.[25] The war, said Frederick Douglass, was "now invested with sanctity."[26]

Moreover, the proclamation announced the acceptance of black men into the Union Army and Navy, enabling the liberated to become liberators. It further ordered that Union officers had no duty to return slaves to their masters. By the end of the war nearly half a million slaves had escaped their masters and made their way to the safety of Northern territories. At first blacks were allowed only to fill support roles, but as pressure increased it was determined that they might be effective in combat. And once given the chance, nearly two hundred thousand black soldiers and sailors fought heroically for the Union and for freedom. In fact, the Bureau of Colored Troops was established to manage the exploding number of soldiers. Lincoln came to agree with Frederick Douglass, who said, "Once let the black man get upon his person the brass letters, U.S., let him get an eagle on his button, and a musket on his shoulder and bullets in his pocket, there is no power on earth that can deny that he has earned the right to citizenship."[27] As the historian Edna Greene Medford observed, "The Emancipation alone may not have been enough to embolden these black men to seek the rights of other citizens, but its very existence doubtless helped to steel their resolve to do so. It gave them hope that full inclusion in American society was a dream about to be realized."[28]

Despite its limitations, the Emancipation Proclamation marked the high point of the Civil War. It became a landmark in human progress—it was the beginning of the end of slavery in the United States; it changed the whole nature of the war and made it, at least in part, a crusade for human freedom. It gave hope and encouragement to those wishing to advance freedom in America and throughout the world. Although it was initially justified by a military necessity to preserve the Union, the true genius of the Emancipation Proclamation was that it worked at a number of levels. Viewed only as a war measure, the proclamation created confusion in the South and deprived the Confederacy of vital manpower. It encouraged the rush of black refugees into Union lines and stimulated military action as white soldiers learned to deal, slowly but steadily, with new brothers-in-arms. Seen as a diplomatic document, it succeeded in rallying to the Northern cause thousands of British and European laborers who were eager to see workers gain their freedom in America and around the world. As a humanitarian document, the proclamation gave hope to millions of African Americans, and renewed the faith of civil rights crusaders who championed the causes of dignity and freedom. By galvanizing abolition forces in many places, it helped prepare the way for the final eradication of slavery by constitutional amendment. Lincoln had found a way to unite those who fought for their country while simultaneously fulfilling his personal ambition to strike a blow at the hated institution of slavery.

Lincoln's proclamation electrified the world. It irrevocably committed the government of the United States to the termination of slavery. It was an act of political courage, taken at the right time, in the right way. Recognized as an enduring symbol of freedom, the proclamation is Lincoln's greatest legacy. Back in 1841, Lincoln had told his friend Joshua Speed that "he had done nothing to make any human being remember that he had lived." Lincoln's ultimate ambition was to "link his name with something that would redound to the interest of his fellow man." Speed reminded Lincoln of that conversation after he had issued the Emancipation Proclamation. Lincoln said, "I believe that in this measure my fondest hopes will be realized."[29]

5

Lincoln and Total War

And so the dreadful massacre began;
O'er fields and orchards, and o'er woodland crests,
the ceaseless fusillade of terror ran.

—Henry Wadsworth Longfellow

On July 7, 1862, General George McClellan, commander of the Army of the Potomac, wrote a letter to his commander in chief from his encampment near Harrison's Landing, Virginia. His purpose was to set forth his views on the state of the rebellion, and to articulate those convictions "deeply impressed upon my mind and my heart." The war, wrote McClellan,

> should be conducted upon the highest principles known to Christian Civilization. It should not be a War upon population; but against armed forces. . . . Neither confiscation of property . . . nor forcible abolition of slavery should be contemplated for a moment.[1]

McClellan's letter neatly summarized the federal government's position as the war commenced in 1861. The aim was to preserve the Union by putting down the rebel insurrection quickly and efficiently. Lincoln, therefore, advocated a policy of limited war, insisting that the conflict be kept within clearly defined bounds. Erring secessionist states were to be taken back into the Union, and Southern society was not to be reshaped. The authority of the national government was to be reestablished by respecting, not abusing, the constitutional rights of the rebels. Notwithstanding radicals in the North who pushed for emancipation, the limited war concept would satisfy the general populace as long as reasonable progress in the field could be shown.

Believers in this limited war strategy hoped that the goals could be met even as the army acted in a humane, professional manner. A harsh, vindictive war would inflame the passions of the rebels and only delay reunion. Better that the army conduct itself, as McClellan's letter shows, as gentlemen. There would be no foraging for food, no destruction of property or interference with property (i.e., slave owners') rights, and no punishment of rebels. The war would be fought between the two armies, McClellan and his subordinates believed, and not against the Southern population. The federals would prevail by methodically building a huge, unbeatable fighting force and then outmaneuvering the Confederates. "The object is not to fight great battles, and storm impregnable fortifications," said Union general Don Carlos Buell, "but by demonstrations and maneuvering to prevent the enemy from concentrating his scattered forces."[2] Lincoln agreed, and hoped that the goal could be met with a minimum of disruption and bloodshed. "In considering the policy to be adopted for suppressing the insurrection," he told Congress in December, "I have been anxious and careful that the inevitable conflict for this purpose shall not degenerate into a violent and remorseless revolutionary struggle."[3]

Within a year, however, it would become painfully apparent to Lincoln that the strategy of limited war would not be successful. His generals fought reluctantly or, even worse, incompetently against their Confederate counterparts. The patience of the Northern populace wore thin, and criticism from politicians of both parties and from the press increased. Out of necessity Lincoln took on a more active role in managing the war, formulating strategy, influencing movements, and supervising the fields of operations. Lincoln searched desperately for generals who could lead troops aggressively. Finally it became clear that the limited war would have to be replaced by total war, and that that policy, carried out by Ulysses S. Grant and William Tecumseh Sherman, would eventually bring about the destruction of the Confederacy.

Lincoln's initial willingness to refrain from involving himself directly with strategic matters seemed prudent. His only military experience was a brief period of undistinguished duty in the Black Hawk War of 1832, where his popularity with local men earned him the rank of captain, and where he muddled through a series of misadventures, none involving combat. At the outset of the war Lincoln believed that the Southern insurgency would be stifled within a few months, perhaps a year. He ordered a blockade of Southern ports (a move that proved to be an effective use of Union naval superiority), and he called for 75,000 voluntary enlistments to serve for ninety days (a number that would become pitifully inadequate). Aside from his insistence that the city of Washington be defended at all costs, Lincoln made no other direct strategic decisions. He believed that the force he had called for could be effectively managed and deployed, and that in those matters it was "his duty to defer" to his military leaders, namely, General Winfield Scott and his replacement, George McClellan.[4]

But both men proved to be woefully ineffective. At age seventy-five, Scott was well past his prime. He suffered from vertigo and gout and was so overweight that he could not mount a horse. A hero of the Mexican War, Scott had served as the nation's general-in-chief for two decades. Though he initially favored compromise on the secession issue, a position Lincoln could

never accept, he had successfully ensured that Lincoln's inauguration proceeded peacefully, and he was zealously loyal to the president. Now, for Lincoln, he devised his "Anaconda Plan," a
strategy whereby a naval blockade would choke off Confederate
supplies in the east while the Union Army gradually built up
strength and secured the Mississippi River in the west. The plan
was derided in the press and for the most part dismissed by War
Department officials, mainly because it was considered to be
overly cautious and did not call for a direct invasion into rebel
territory. After a series of early Union losses, including the battles
of Bull Run and Ball's Bluff, Scott resigned in November 1861.
(The Anaconda Plan, however, would ultimately prove to be a
successful strategy; eventually all its parts would be implemented
to some degree by Union armies.)

McClellan was given every chance to prove his worth in two
separate command stints, but his agonizing tactics of delay
proved to be more than the patient Lincoln could bear. McClellan was an intelligent young man, an engineer and West Point
graduate, who excelled at military organization and preparation.
As general-in-chief he proved to be a relentless drillmaster but a
tentative fighter at best. Tempered by his experiences in the Mexican War and buoyed by some minor successes in western Virginia in the summer of 1861, McClellan was hampered by a huge
ego. He disdained civilian leadership, resented any advice that
was offered, and was openly critical of Lincoln, the cabinet, and
members of Congress. He was guilty of regularly overestimating
the strength of the enemy. Preferring to drill his soldiers rather
then press the battle, McClellan was loved by his men but was a
constant source of frustration to the White House. The general
was a proslavery Democrat, but Lincoln chose to overlook political differences and trusted that McClellan would eventually devise a workable military plan.

After months of delay McClellan finally settled on a strategy
that called for an attack on the Confederate capital of Richmond

from the east. But once the campaign commenced he fought defensively and continued to complain that he had not been given enough soldiers. He was baffled by Confederate movements and could not countermove. Relations between him and Lincoln grew increasingly sour. McClellan fretted about the loss of Union lives, and his insecurities about his soldiers' readiness and the size of the enemy led to more procrastination. He could never bring himself to accept responsibility, but was quick to blame others, including subordinates and officials in Washington. He wrote the secretary of war: "You have done your best to sacrifice this army," but the telegraph operator deleted the sentence from the rest of the message.

Weary of dealing with overly cautious commanders, and facing increased criticism from Congress and in the press (particularly after the disaster at Bull Run), in 1862 Lincoln began to take a far more active role in managing military affairs. He read books on military theory, consulted with his advisers, and carefully studied maps and organizational charts. He requested information as to the location of forces, their state of readiness, and the levels of arms and ammunition they held. These efforts enabled Lincoln to begin to formulate a basic war strategy in his own mind. He would never again adhere to the position that a passive containment strategy would suffice to bring the Confederates to their senses and win the war. The war would have to be *fought* if it was to be won, and Lincoln intended to win it.[5] He came to realize the wisdom of Scott's idea for securing the Mississippi Valley, and thereafter his strategic outlines stressed success in the western as well as eastern theaters. Recognizing that the Union had the advantage in numbers and in weapons production capabilities, Lincoln believed that the Union troops should "threaten all their positions at the same time and with superior force, and if they weakened one to strengthen another, seize and hold the one weakened."[6] He was becoming the military's commander in chief, and he was progressing from administrator to war president.

In January 1862 Lincoln fired the corrupt and ineffective secretary of war Simon Cameron for personal and professional reasons. Cameron was "selfish and openly discourteous," Lincoln said
privately. And since he had proven himself to be "incapable of either organizing details or conceiving and advising general plans,"
his service was "obnoxious to the Country."[7] Lincoln replaced
Cameron with Edwin Stanton, a serious, capable man with the
will to succeed. Stanton was dedicated, honest, and efficient, and
his energetic efforts would soon revitalize the War Department
and bring much-needed direction to the Union military effort.

Next, Lincoln issued General War Order Number One, which
called for all Union armies to advance no later than February 22.
The order was unrealistic and eventually withdrawn before it
could be ignored by McClellan, but it gave an indication of Lincoln's resolve for action. Lincoln also ordered governmental control
of the U.S. telegraph system, establishing direct communication
between his office and the generals in the field. For the rest of the
war Lincoln was a regular visitor to the War Department's telegraph office, sending and receiving messages, following movements
as they occurred, and monitoring progress (or lack of progress) in
the various theaters. He told his commanders that he would not
be satisfied with the mere occupation of Confederate territories;
he wanted to aggressively carry the war to the South and defeat its
armies. And in April, when Major General David Hunter declared
Georgia, Florida, and South Carolina to be under martial law and
ordered their slaves emancipated, Lincoln rescinded Hunter's order, saying that decision was reserved for himself as president. "I
cannot feel justified," Lincoln wrote, "in leaving [this] decision to
commanders in the field."[8] He was growing into his job.

In 1862 Lincoln's theory of a coordinated, simultaneous attack
on all fronts began to produce mixed results. The military theaters of operations, now divided geographically and headed by
main field commanders, were located in Tennessee, northern Virginia, and the Mississippi River. In central Tennessee in October,

the Confederates under Braxton Bragg fought Buell's Army of the Cumberland to a draw at Perryville, and then retreated; Buell's failure to pursue cost him his command. Major General William Rosecrans replaced Buell as head of the federals and in late December 1862 met Bragg at Stones River. Again brutal fighting took place, and again Bragg retreated. While the tactical victory boosted Union morale, Rosecrans delayed his pursuit until June, squandering another opportunity to crush the rebels. Still, Lincoln was pleased that the Union had taken effective control of Tennessee.

Chaos seemed to prevail in Virginia, however. McClellan's Army of the Potomac fought cautiously at Fair Oaks, and then again during the Seven Days battles, in June. As if to justify his lack of aggression, in early July McClellan delivered to Lincoln, from Harper's Landing, his letter regarding limited, humane war. In August he failed to reinforce John Pope's army at the Second Battle of Bull Run, but it was Pope who was chastised and not McClellan. Finally McClellan earned a victory at Antietam in September—providing Lincoln the opportunity to announce his emancipation timetable—but drew Lincoln's wrath when, citing fatigue and overextension of his forces, he failed to chase and destroy Robert E. Lee's army. Lincoln finally had had enough and relieved McClellan of his duties in November 1862, barely one year into his command. Since McClellan was not using his army, Lincoln sarcastically noted, "he would like to borrow it" for a while.

Now under Ambrose Burnside, the army moved toward Richmond but was crushed at Fredericksburg in a one-sided disaster for the Union. Desperate for a leader who could inspire his men and fight aggressively, Lincoln named yet another major general, Joseph Hooker, to head the Army of the Potomac. Hooker had been an ambitious corps commander but also had a reputation for drunkenness and insubordination. He also encouraged a bevy of women of relaxed morals to follow his troops—perhaps an effort to build morale. These women became known as "Hookers"—a dubious concession to the general and a title that has endured. He had suggested, after Fredericksburg, that the nation needed a dictator. In response, Lincoln wrote, "Only those generals that gain successes, can set up dictators. What I now ask of you is military success, and I will risk the dictatorship. The government will support you to the utmost of its ability, which is neither more nor less than it has done and will do for all commanders. . . . Beware of rashness, but with energy, and sleepless vigilance, go forward, and give us victories."[9]

At one point Lincoln became so irritated over the failure of his generals to press the war against the Confederate forces even when the enemy was in retreat that he seriously considered going into the field and commanding one of the Union armies himself. In a cooler moment he recognized that as president he had numerous other duties that would be neglected if he went off to war. But Lincoln was a superb commander in chief whose leadership in that role was a major reason why the Union was to win the war. His judgment and leadership were far superior to that of the Confederate president, Jefferson Davis.

Meanwhile, goaded and pressured by Lincoln, Union forces were meeting with success in the West, where Major General Ulysses S. Grant was determined to control the Mississippi Valley. A West Point graduate, Grant had given up his commission in 1854 only to fail at a variety of civilian careers, and when war came in 1861 he had jumped at the chance to again wear the uniform. To the relief of Lincoln and the delight of Northern newspapers, Grant's aggressive actions produced victories. In the Tennessee Valley, he took Forts Henry and Donelson, capturing nearly fifteen hundred rebel prisoners (at Donelson he famously demanded "unconditional surrender"), and then secured Nashville and Memphis. Surprised at Shiloh, Grant suffered horrendous losses but managed to hang on. He dressed casually, ignored basic Army protocol, and liked to drink bourbon whiskey. But Lincoln deflected any criticism away from Grant. "I can't spare this man," he said. "He fights."

Reportedly when Lincoln was informed of Grant's drinking habits, the president said: "Find out what he's drinking and order it for my other generals."

Grant continued to show his mettle by taking Vicksburg. He recognized (as Lincoln did) that control of that city was crucial to supply and troop movement along the Mississippi River. Vicksburg was heavily fortified by Confederate guns; Lincoln said that the war could not end until "that key is in our pocket."[10] Grant maneuvered his men into position by crossing the Mississippi below Vicksburg, then forced the enemy into defensive positions and relentlessly attacked. Taking advantage of Lincoln's directive that authorized Union commanders to "seize and use any property, real or personal, which may be necessary or convenient . . . for supplies or other military purposes," Grant allowed his soldiers to forage for food, taking what they could from the surrounding countryside, rebel farms, and plantations.[11] Meanwhile, Union forces fired on the city day and night, trapping both Confederate soldiers and citizens. With the fall of Vicksburg, the Union now controlled the entire Mississippi Valley, and Lincoln knew he had found the leader he had been looking for. Lincoln called Grant's strategy "one of the most brilliant in the world," and said, "Grant is my man and I am his for the rest of the war."[12]

Lincoln admitted surprise that Southern resistance, even in the wake of scattered Union victories, remained so strong, and he now realized that this popular resistance had to be conquered. Grant's success absolutely convinced Lincoln that only a hard-hitting, no-holds-barred offense on a wide front could break the resistance of the South. A new military strategy would be implemented.[13] Grant's relentless offensive techniques, and his willingness to take what he needed to improve his chances of victory, would become the model for the entire Union Army. Lincoln moved to a strategy of total war. This was no longer a match between two armies. Anyone, or anything, that contributed to the Southern war effort was now fair game.

John Pope was one of the chief architects of Lincoln's new vision. Pope had met with success in the West and had been promoted to major general despite a reputation for braggadocio and pettiness toward his superior officers. But Lincoln liked his aggressiveness and appointed him to lead the new Army of Virginia, which had been organized from scattered forces along the Shenandoah Valley and was meant to supplant McClellan's failed policies. On July 14, 1862, Pope delivered an address to his new soldiers, who, having been led previously by the cautious McClellan, were astonished at the tone of his words. "Let us understand each other," Pope said. "I have come to you from the West, where we have always seen the backs of our enemies; from an army whose business it has been to seek the adversary and to beat him when he was found; whose policy has been attack and not defense. . . . I have been called here to pursue the same system and to lead you against the enemy. It is my purpose to do so, and that speedily. I am sure you long for an opportunity to win the distinction you are capable of achieving. That opportunity I shall endeavor to give you."[14] As Grant and Henry W. Halleck had ordered in the West, Pope now allowed his men to forage for foodstuffs, goods, and supplies wherever they might be found on enemy soil. They were authorized to seize private property without providing compensation, to punish or expel civilians who refused to take oaths of loyalty, and even to execute captured rebel irregulars. Northern opinion backed these tactics of aggressive warfare. But for all his bravado, Pope was no match for Robert E. Lee and found himself hopelessly outmaneuvered throughout the summer. He was relieved of his command in September, and McClellan was given another chance to lead.

But 1863 brought new struggles for the Army of the Potomac. Because that army was based close to Washington, Lincoln was able to more closely monitor its actions and movements. Occasionally he visited his commanders in the field. But he could only watch helplessly as they continued to demonstrate ineptitude and timidity. In May, Union forces under Hooker met with the smaller rebel army at Chancellorsville and were soundly defeated. "My God," Lincoln repeated over and over. "What will the country say?" Robert E. Lee then seized the momentum and invaded Pennsylvania, hoping to further demoralize the Northern public by capturing a large Union city, perhaps the capital itself.

Desperately in search of a general who could match Lee in a fight, in late June, Lincoln named George Meade to head the Army of the Potomac—the fifth general to do so. Days later Meade engaged Lee at Gettysburg, and, taking advantage of Lee's uncharacteristic bungling, crippled the rebel army in three bloody days of fighting. But when Lee retreated back to Virginia, Meade inexplicably failed to pursue him. Meade was satisfied that the enemy had been driven from Union soil, but Lincoln seethed that another opportunity to smash Lee once and for all had been lost. His anger at Meade's letting Lee escape, noted a friend, was "something sorrowful to behold."[15]

Although his generals met with only mixed success in the field, Lincoln became more and more convinced of the justification for total war, and that it must be carried through no matter the cost. In November 1863 he traveled by train to Gettysburg for the dedication of a new national Soldiers Cemetery on the site of the battlefield. His remarks on November 19 were not the main event of the afternoon; that honor belonged to famed orator Edward Everett, who preceded Lincoln and spoke for two hours. But Lincoln's two-minute address remains his most famous speech, and perhaps the most beloved in American history. For Lincoln did far more than simply honor those soldiers who had given their lives for their country. He succeeded in redefining the very meaning of the war itself. The struggle was no longer simply over the survival of the Union, Lincoln said, but for the ideals of freedom promised for all Americans in the Declaration of Independence. In that sense freedom was reborn, and the world itself would take note. The country, indivisible, was not merely a collection of states but a *nation*, "conceived in liberty, and dedicated to the proposition that all men are created equal." Men had fallen so that the republic would live, and now was the opportunity for the living to ensure that "this nation, under God, shall have a new birth of freedom and that government of the people, by the people, for the people shall not perish from the earth."

Lincoln declared that day: "The world will little note, nor long remember what we say here, but it can never forget what they did here. It is for us the living, rather, to be dedicated here to the unfinished work which they who fought here have thus far so nobly advanced."

No one can understand the greatness of Lincoln in his own time and in his place in history without reading some of his great speeches. Most of these addresses were carefully constructed by Lincoln—sometimes over periods of days or weeks, even months. He drew on extensive reading of the works of men he admired—Henry Clay, Daniel Webster, George Washington, Thomas Jefferson. He kept on his writing desk copies of his own speeches that provided lines and ideas he might work into the speech at hand.

Lincoln frequently pulled passages out of the King James version of the Bible, from the Hebrew prophets of the Old Testament and from Christ and his disciples in the New Testament. He borrowed ideas from Shakespeare, Robert Burns, *Aesop's Fables*, and John Bunyan's *The Pilgrim's Progress*. He also drew from his experiences growing up in Kentucky and Indiana and from his legislative and lawyerly years in Illinois. His mind and his command of diction were doubtless sharpened in his debates with his able, experienced opponent Senator Stephen Douglas.

After penning a first draft of a speech, he would often ask a trusted friend or associate, or in later years a member of his cabinet—especially Secretary of State William Seward—to critically read what he had written. In some instances he would read his speech aloud to a critic and then listen while the critic read it aloud.

Prior to the speech at Gettysburg, Lincoln had delivered four speeches that could be described as great: his speech against the Kansas-Nebraska Act in Peoria, Illinois, on October 16, 1854; his acceptance of the Republican nomination for the U.S. Senate race against Stephen Douglas at Springfield, Illinois, on June 16, 1858 (the "house divided" speech); his speech at New York City's Cooper Union on February 27, 1860; and his first inaugural address as president, on March 4, 1861. His second inaugural address, delivered on March 4, 1865, was also deserving of the description "great"—some would say it was his greatest speech.

But it is the Gettysburg Address, although brief, that has lived in history as an enduring political and literary treasure. Its fame places it alongside the Declaration of Independence and the Bill of Rights. Indeed, over the years more teachers and students have learned to recite the Gettysburg Address than any other document in American history. For it is in its 272 words that Lincoln redefined the meaning of the Union and of the sacrifice that had sanctified its preservation.

Lincoln was the most masterful speechwriter of any president in our national history. Much of his success in the American political arena derived from his superior ability to draft compelling public addresses. Likewise, his high place in history rests heavily on his beautiful prose. He was a literary giant.

A recently published book by Douglas L. Wilson entitled *Lincoln's Sword: The Presidency and the Power of Words* offers a clear picture of Lincoln's methodology in the writing of speeches, letters, and essays. The author leaves little doubt that Lincoln was in a literary class above all other presidents. Perhaps Jefferson and Wilson would rank numbers two and three.

As the war dragged on into its fourth year, there was plenty of hard fighting left to do. By 1864 Lincoln, satisfied that Grant's vision of warfare coincided with his own, wanted to put Grant in charge of the entire Union Army. But Grant was not eager to leave the western theater. In February 1864 a bill was introduced in Congress reviving the rank of lieutenant general and designating the recipient as supreme commander of all the Union armies. Weeks later Lincoln met Grant for the first time and awarded him his new commission. He also insisted that Grant come east; public pressure and practical necessity demanded it. Grant agreed when Lincoln promised him unfettered control. Sherman took Grant's old position as head of the Army of the Cumberland in the East. Meade would technically lead the Army of the Potomac, but Grant was determined to ride with the army in the field. He wanted no part of a Washington office job, he insisted. He would communicate with other generals via the telegraph. Halleck would act as a go-between, relaying orders and information and keeping Lincoln and Stanton informed as events unfolded.

With Lincoln's firm approval, Grant devised a grand strategy whereby Union armies would move in concert along a thousand-mile front from Virginia to Louisiana. Grant, Meade, and the Army of the Potomac would aggressively pursue Lee and force him back to Richmond; General Benjamin Butler's Army of the James was to move toward Petersburg; and William Sherman, who had succeeded Grant as head of the Union armies in the West, would lead his hundred thousand soldiers through Georgia with the aim of capturing Atlanta. This simultaneous advance was meant to exert relentless, maximum pressure at different places at the same time, exposing rebel weaknesses and resulting in inevitable breakthroughs. The plan utilized the overwhelming strength and numbers of the Union Army. "Those not skinning can hold a leg," joked Lincoln.[16]

Grant took the offensive during the terrible, bloody campaign of 1864. With an army numbering some 120,000 men he crossed Virginia's Rapidan River into the Wilderness, a region named for thick forestation and dense underbrush. In May he met Lee's forces, who, although greatly outnumbered, thwarted Grant's attack. Unlike his predecessors, Grant did not retreat but flanked

Lee's army and engaged it again, a week later at Spotsylvania Court House and then at Cold Harbor. For a month the two armies clashed. The Union suffered nearly sixty thousand casualties; the Confederates, twenty thousand. The public was appalled at the carnage, and Lincoln was heartbroken. He knew the truth of the brutal strategy, however; the North could continually resupply its army, while the enemy had little or nothing in reserve. All but dismissing the horrific loss of life, Grant relentlessly pushed the battle. He advanced toward Petersburg, just twenty miles from Richmond, and dug in, surrounding Lee's army. The resulting siege would last ten months.

While Grant kept Lee occupied in Virginia, Sherman's forces in the West flexed their muscles, embarking from Chattanooga and proceeding southward, engaging the army of General Joseph Johnston and later that of John Bell Hood. In his march Sherman was generally victorious in a series of some nineteen battles, often in and around mountainous terrain, taking advantage of superior numbers and a steady stream of reinforcements. Sherman enthusiastically embraced the Lincoln/Grant strategy of total war, which he called "hard war." He knew that it was not enough to defeat the rebel army; the Confederates' economic ability to wage war had to be dismantled as well. The will of the Southern people had to be broken; their spirit had to be crushed. "We are not only fighting hostile armies but a hostile people, and must make old and young, rich and poor, feel the hard hand of war," he said.[17] The war would now be conducted as a conquest.

Sherman advanced through Georgia at a frantic pace, applying "scorched earth" tactics as he went. His army was authorized to destroy civilian supplies and foodstuffs. It burned fields, tore up rail lines, and wrecked the state's infrastructure. The looting of homes was officially forbidden, but offenders were not punished or even chastised by their commanders. Sherman was in a hurry to accomplish his goals. "If you can whip Lee and I can march to the Atlantic I think ol' Uncle Abe will give us twenty days leave to see the young folks," he cheerily wrote to Grant as the campaign commenced.[18]

Sherman captured Atlanta on September 2, 1864, an accomplishment that lionized his name in the North and did much to ensure Lincoln's reelection two months later. After ordering civilians to evacuate the city, Sherman ordered it burned to the ground. He would, he said, "make Georgia howl," and he delivered on his promise. Now promoted to major general, he kept pushing south and east toward Savannah in his relentless "march to the sea." His men were ruthless in the destruction of Southern property, causing an estimated $100 million in damages. Sherman's name would be forever vilified in the South, but he explained his actions this way:

> You cannot qualify war in harsher terms than I will. War is cruelty, and you cannot refine it; and those who brought war into our country deserve all the curses and maledictions a people can pour out. I know I had no hand in making this war, and I know I will make more sacrifices to-day than any of you to secure peace. But you cannot have peace and a division of our country. If the United States submits to a division now, it will not stop, but will go on until we reap the fate of Mexico, which is eternal war. . . . I want peace, and believe it can only be reached through union and war, and I will ever conduct war with a view to perfect and early success.[19]

Major Henry Hitchcock, a member of Sherman's staff, also justified the tactics. "It is a terrible thing to consume and destroy the sustenance of thousands of people," he said. But if hard war served "to paralyze their husbands and fathers who are fighting . . . it is mercy in the end."[20] It was particularly devastating in South Carolina, where Unionists believed the rebellion began. Sherman's soldiers terrorized Southerners deliberately. He had a terrible power, he said, and "I intended to use it . . . to humble their pride, to follow them to their inmost recesses, and to make them fear and dread us. . . . We cannot change the hearts and minds of those people of the south, but we can make war so terrible, and make them so sick of war that generations would pass away before they would again appeal to it." Federal soldiers agreed. "Here is where the treason began," said one man, "and, by God, here is where it shall end."[21] Now it would be only a matter of time. Little wonder that Sherman uttered the reflection that has often been quoted even today: "War is hell."

Lincoln's remarkable military leadership—one of his greatest achievements—makes one wonder how the Union forces could have prevailed without him. He was truly commander in chief in the best sense of the title. Knowledgeable about every aspect of the war, he understood the weaknesses and strengths of every general. He did not hesitate to replace an officer after a blown assignment. He came to the firm conviction early in the war that the army must aggressively carry the war to the opposing army. If the enemy retreated, Lincoln insisted that the Union general in charge, instead of resting, should pursue the routed force and destroy them.

After 1861, Lincoln never wavered in his conviction that, given the North's advantage in numbers of men, weapons, railways, and industrial resources, Union forces should press forward all across the lines of battle, hitting the Southern army in all theaters simultaneously. This strategy would prevent Southern generals from moving forces from places not under attack to those that were under attack. McClellan and other Northern generals, educated at West Point, were taught the strategies that had worked in previous wars in North America and Europe. But like American officers of the twentieth century who had to learn that the military methods of World Wars I and II would not work in Vietnam or Iraq, Lincoln and his officers found that the methods of George Washington were not effective against the Southern rebellion.

Lincoln's success in winning the war is all the more remarkable in that most of his generals were largely mediocre, including McClellan, Burnside, Hooker, Meade, Buell, Halleck, and Rosecrans. The historian T. Harry Williams concludes that "the only Civil War generals who deserve to be marked as great are Lee for the South and Grant and Sherman for the North."[22]

A century after the Civil War, the historian Shelby Foote visited two great-granddaughters of the Confederate general Nathan Bedford Forrest at their home in South Carolina. Thinking to score a point with the aging sisters, he told them that the Civil War had produced two geniuses: their great-grandfather in the South and Abraham Lincoln in the North. Well, replied one of the sisters, we don't think much of Mr. Lincoln around here![23]

Notwithstanding this evaluation by a loyal daughter of the Confederacy, Lincoln's masterful direction of the Union forces, in spite of his scant military experience, marks him as a commander truly worthy of the label "genius." As the scholar James Ford Rhodes concluded many years ago, "The preponderating asset of the North proved to be Lincoln."[24]

6

Politics in Wartime

Why should there not be a patient confidence in the ultimate justice of the people? Is there any better or equal hope in the world?
—Abraham Lincoln, First Inaugural Address, 1861

Abraham Lincoln believed that free and regular elections were the very foundation of the republic, and despite the gruesome war that savaged the country and divided the people, he was determined that the 1864 election should proceed in as orderly a fashion as possible. While some in Washington whispered that the election should be canceled or postponed, Lincoln saw it as an opportunity—indeed, a necessity—for the country to carry on while struggling so mightily with disunion. And Lincoln wanted very much to serve a second term as president. He considered it his duty to finish the business of winning the war, and he meant to fulfill his pledges to preserve the Union and ensure freedom for all Americans. But to gain a second term Lincoln had to withstand challenges from dissenters within his own party and from a determined Democratic opposition, while at the same time convincing skeptics that he possessed the necessary qualities to lead the country to a better day. He had to persuade a war-weary public that victory on the battlefield was within sight, and he had to engage in some hardball politics as well.

But political precedent seemed to be against him. Not since Andrew Jackson in 1832 had an incumbent president been re-elected; in fact, only one man, Martin Van Buren, had been nominated for reelection by his party, and he had been soundly defeated by William Henry Harrison in 1840. Further, in the 1862 elections the Republicans had managed to pick up two seats in the Senate but lost twenty-two in the House of Representatives. Federal failures in the war along with at best mixed reaction to the issuance of the Emancipation Proclamation had caused Lincoln's popularity to sink. Back home in Springfield, Lincoln's former law partner John T. Stuart, a Democrat, defeated the Republican incumbent for Lincoln's old seat in Congress.

The situation had improved, if only temporarily, over the summer and fall of 1863. Lincoln's armies had achieved important, if costly, success on several fronts. Lee had been defeated at Gettysburg, and while he had not been crushed as Lincoln had hoped, he had at least been driven back to Southern soil, his invasion plans ruined. In the West, Grant's army had scored impressive victories at Vicksburg and Chattanooga, opening up the Mississippi River and establishing control of the state of Tennessee. The blockade around Southern ports along the Atlantic coast continued to choke Confederate supply lines and discourage European intervention on behalf of the rebels. When Republicans captured important governorships in Pennsylvania and Ohio in the November elections, Lincoln had reason for optimism as 1864 began.

But bickering and dissension ran through the Republican Party (now officially called the National Union Party) and threatened to derail Lincoln's hopes for another nomination. The radical element of the party—led by Charles Sumner, Thaddeus Stevens, Owen Lovejoy, and Elihu Washburne—ceaselessly clamored for abolition and were not impressed with Lincoln's limited Emancipation Proclamation. Lincoln simply had never been presidential material, they charged. He was lazy and indecisive, lacking the respect of Congress and the public.

Others saw him as deficient in style and professional conduct, shortcomings that were reflected in the clumsy way he was handling the war. They believed that Lincoln was too slow to support black soldiers in their efforts to secure their civil rights and opportunities. Sumner said that while at the core Lincoln was undoubtedly a good man, he "lacked practical talent," and it was a tragedy "to have the power of a god and not use it godlike."[1]

Senator Lyman Trumbull of Illinois spoke for many Republicans in Washington when he said, "You would be surprised, in talking with public men we meet here, to find how few, when you come to get at their real sentiments, are for Mr. Lincoln's reelection. There is a distrust and fear that he is too undecided and inefficient to put down the rebellion."[2] Many Republicans longed for a stronger, more mature candidate in 1864 who could lead the country out of what they saw as Lincoln's disaster.

Radicals believed that the man the country so desperately needed could be found in Lincoln's cabinet: Secretary of the Treasury Salmon P. Chase. It was no secret that Chase, the man the *New York Herald* called "the Moses of the radicals," aspired to be president; in fact, he believed he had been born for the job.[3] He had "never forgiven Lincoln" for securing the Republican nomination in 1860 and still could barely believe that the country had elected Lincoln president.[4] Studious and highly intelligent, Chase had been an efficient Treasury secretary, but his skills at financing the war were perhaps overshadowed by his personal ambition and constant scheming. He feuded with Secretary of State William Seward and sought the endorsement of the *New York Tribune*'s Horace Greeley. Chase resented Lincoln's self-reliance, for he was convinced that he was morally and intellectually superior to Lincoln. He lacked humility; Senator Ben Wade joked that Chase believed he was the "fourth person in the Trinity."[5] Chase had tendered his resignation at least three times in three years, always over some perceived slight, but it had been rejected each time; Lincoln needed a man of Chase's abilities in the cabinet, and he also wanted to keep an eye on him politically.

It was a poorly kept secret that Chase's supporters had mobilized for a run at the White House. In December 1863 a group calling itself the "Organization to Make S. P. Chase President"—the membership list included governors, senators, generals, and even the vice president, Hannibal Hamlin—met in Washington and organized campaign committees. Within two months the group had drafted and distributed, at taxpayer expense, a hundred thousand copies of a document titled "The Next Presidential Election." The document stated that Lincoln was unfit for reelection as he was "the real cause of why our well-appointed armies have not succeeded in the destruction of the rebellion."[6] A second document, released in February and named the Pomeroy Circular after its author, Senator Samuel Pomeroy of Kansas, called for Chase to be the country's next president.

In times when it was considered unseemly for anyone to publicly announce his candidacy (and doubly so when the announcement might come at the expense of the sitting president), Chase feigned outrage at the circular. He denied any knowledge of its contents and immediately offered Lincoln another resignation, which was once again refused. But now Congressman Francis Blair of Missouri, a former Union general and the brother of Postmaster General Montgomery Blair, went on the offensive against Chase. With no objection from Lincoln, Blair vigorously attacked Chase on the House floor, accusing the Treasury Department of fraud and corruption and calling for a complete investigation of Chase's office. Although the investigation never materialized, the National Union Party in Chase's home state of Ohio passed a resolution endorsing Lincoln's renomination. Soon Chase's friends advised him to withdraw his name from the contest, and he grudgingly agreed.

Chase's candidacy, white-hot and gaining momentum just months earlier, had now been extinguished.

The radicals had to look elsewhere for an alternative to Lincoln. Former Union commander John C. Frémont, the party's first nominee for president in 1856, presented an intriguing possibility. Frémont was a strong abolitionist who, as officer in charge of the Army's Western Department, had declared martial law in Missouri in 1861, confiscated rebel property, and emancipated slaves. Afraid the moves would cause Missouri to join the Confederacy, Lincoln had revoked Frémont's directives and removed him from command. Three years later Frémont found himself back in politics, seeking to take the nomination from a president he did not respect. Radicals calculated that Frémont would attract antislavery societies in the Midwest and New England, as well as disappointed Chase supporters.

But this group was far too small to take control of the National Union Party. Instead it organized a "People's Convention" in Cleveland in May and adopted a platform that called for a constitutional amendment to end slavery. It also endorsed the confiscation of rebel property and declared that reconstruction was the province of Congress, not the president. Though Frémont would eventually prove to be an uninspired candidate, Lincoln worried that he might steal votes from him and sought ways to get him to withdraw. In September, Senator Zachariah Chandler of Michigan negotiated a deal: Frémont would withdraw from the race if Lincoln would remove Montgomery Blair, whose partisan activities in the Chase matter had angered many radicals, from his cabinet. Lincoln agreed, and on September 22 Frémont took himself out of the running.

Another army commander, none other than General Ulysses S. Grant himself, was the choice of many to head the Republican ticket. Grant's most significant backer was James Gordon Bennett, the editor of the *New York Herald*. "It is evident that our next President must be a military man of tried experience and acknowledged capacity," wrote Bennett. "We have had quite enough of a Civilian Commander-in-chief during the past four years."[7] Grant's popularity was such that he had been approached by Democratic Party officials the previous winter, who inquired if he was interested in running for president. "That question astonishes me," Grant said in response. "I do not know of anything I have ever said or done which would indicate that I would be a candidate for any office whatever within the gift of the people. . . . Nothing likely to happen would pain me so much as to see my name used in connection with a political office. I am not a candidate for any office nor for favors from any party." Now that the Radical Republicans were interested, Grant was even more firm in his position. "Nothing would induce me to think of being a presidential candidate," he said, "particularly so long as there is a possibility of having Mr. Lincoln re-elected."[8] Lincoln was gratified to learn of Grant's loyalty and his lack of political aspirations. "No man knows," Lincoln said, "when that presidential grub gets to gnawing at him, just how deep it will get until he has tried it; and I didn't know but what there was one gnawing at Grant."[9] Lincoln was perhaps less worried about Grant as a political opponent than concerned that he might lose the one commander in the field who was up to the task of fighting. Newly christened a lieutenant general—the first man to hold that rank since George Washington—Grant had been placed in charge of all the Union armies and in May 1864 was back in the field, eager to move against the enemy and confident of success.

While the radicals were struggling, Lincoln's operatives were busy behind the scenes. Loyal supporters like Simon Cameron, Thurlow Weed, and Leonard Swett, among many others, worked tirelessly throughout the winter and spring of 1864 to secure delegates who would commit to Lincoln's renomination. With the Confederate war machine seemingly in crisis, and fringes of the National Union Party struggling to come up with a viable alternate candidate, most of the states seemed a sure thing for Lincoln. But he remained at best cautiously optimistic; he remembered he had not been the favorite to gain the nomination in 1860 but had defeated seemingly more qualified opponents.

The National Union Party held its convention in Baltimore during the first week of June. Many state delegations, including some from the rebellious states of South Carolina and Florida, came through Washington to pay their respects to the president. Some were radicals and found themselves in an awkward situation: they did not support Lincoln's administration but realized that they were unlikely to find a candidate who could replace him. They were stuck, it seemed, with Lincoln. Former Whigs and war Democrats now aligned with the Republicans also stopped by the White House. Many pro-Lincoln delegates also visited with the president, most importantly Senator Edwin D. Morgan of New York, the party's national chairman, who, along with Robert J. Breckinridge of Kentucky, would preside over the convention. Lincoln advised Morgan to carry a message to the convention expressing his support for a constitutional amendment banning slavery. It was an effective attempt by Lincoln to heal some of the rifts that had divided radicals from mainstream Republicans, and it served to solidify his hold on the nomination.

Though there was much grumbling from the various factions that made up the party, in the end Lincoln was nominated overwhelmingly, with only Missouri failing to make it a unanimous selection, casting its twenty-two votes for Grant. The convention also chose a vice president, the Unionist and strong war Democrat Andrew Johnson of Tennessee, to replace Hannibal Hamlin. Though the selection surprised many, Lincoln approved of the move. Hamlin was from Maine, and New England seemed safely for Lincoln. The two men had gotten along personally, but Hamlin had drifted toward the radical wing of the party and disagreed with many of the administration's more conservative racial policies. With reconstruction looming, Lincoln wanted to extend the hand of kindness to the South, and Johnson, who had served as military governor in Tennessee, seemed a good fit.

The platform committee came up with eleven resolutions, which were heartily accepted by the delegates. They included promises to quell the rebellion and punish the rebels; rejection of compromise short of unconditional surrender; the abolition of slavery; support for Lincoln and a purge of cabinet officials who did not support him; economic development, including construction of a transcontinental railroad; and vigorous implementation of the Monroe Doctrine. The planks regarding slavery and the cabinet were meant to mollify the radicals, and the others were extensions, or perhaps affirmations, of present administration policies.

Lincoln heard the news of his nomination via telegraph, and then met with party officials the next day at the White House. He issued a statement that concluded: "I have not permitted myself, gentlemen, to conclude that I am the best man in the country; but I am reminded, in this connection, of a story of an old Dutch farmer, who remarked to a companion once that it was not best to swap horses when crossing streams."[10]

While the Republicans had overcome some political obstacles and achieved a degree of unity in selecting Lincoln as their candidate, the war effort took several turns for the worse during the summer of 1864, and the confidence many felt in the spring quickly faded. Grant became bogged down in Virginia, fighting fiercely but gaining little ground at Cold Harbor, Spotsylvania Court House, and the Wilderness. He suffered nearly sixty thousand casualties in just two months, and the Northern press and public were merciless in their criticism of him and of Lincoln. But unlike his predecessors, Grant did not retreat, instead settling in for a long siege at Petersburg. Restless after weeks of stalled action, Union forces dug a mine shaft and extended it underneath Confederate lines, hoping to set off explosions and cripple the enemy forces. But poor planning and a lack of coordination among Union commanders doomed the plan and resulted in more than five thousand Union casualties and a thousand prisoners taken. Meanwhile, in the Shenandoah Valley, General Jubal Early's rebel army moved menacingly toward Washington, hoping to distract at least a portion of Grant's army and embarrass Unionists in the capital; he was successful on both counts.

Despite the setbacks, Lincoln urged Grant to "hold on with a bull-dog grip, and chew and choke, as much as possible."[11] There could be no other strategy but to apply pressure relentlessly, absorb inevitable losses, and eventually win a war of attrition. A negotiated peace settlement seemed impossible. Lincoln would accept nothing less than restoration of the Union and the abandonment of slavery, terms he knew the Confederacy would never accept. He authorized a series of informal peace talks, all of which he knew would prove fruitless, but he believed that his willingness even to enter into such talks sent the right message to the public.

As the stalemate continued, Lincoln kept a brave public face. He called for half a million more troops and stepped up his efforts to inspire them to fight for the cause. "We accepted this war for an object, a worthy object, and the war will end when that object is attained," he told an audience in Philadelphia. "General Grant is reported to have said, I am going through on this line if it takes all summer. . . . If I shall discover that General Grant and the noble officers and men under him can be greatly facilitated in their work by a sudden pouring forward of men and assistance, will you give them to me? Then I say, stand ready, for I am watching for the chance."[12]

The news from Capitol Hill was disappointing that summer as well. Congress passed the Wade-Davis bill, a stringent plan for reconstruction. Before a Southern state could come back into the Union, the proposed law read, at least 50 percent of its voters had to swear an oath of loyalty to the federal government. Further, the state had to guarantee the civil rights of freed slaves. The bill reflected the radicals' intent to punish the rebels, and it was a response to Lincoln's much milder 10 percent plan. Lincoln vetoed the bill (one of only seven vetoes of his presidency), justifying his action by arguing that it might interfere with reconstruction efforts under way in those sections of the South already occupied by the federal troops. Besides, Lincoln believed, reconstruction was primarily an executive, not a legislative, function. All Democrats, and many radical Republicans, savagely attacked Lincoln over the veto. Much of the press criticized him as well; the *New York Tribune* called Lincoln's action a "studied outrage on the legislative authority."[13]

By late August things looked particularly grim for Lincoln and his political prospects. He was advised by National Union Party officials that as the war news continued to dim, he was losing support in many Northern states, including Illinois. His chances for reelection, so bright just eight months earlier, had faded. On the morning of August 23, Lincoln wrote the following on a sheet of paper in his office: "This morning, as for some days past, it seems exceedingly probable that this administration shall not be elected. Then it will be my duty to so cooperate with the President elect as to save the Union between the election and the inauguration, as he will have secured this election on such ground that he cannot save it afterwards." Lincoln folded the note so that its contents could not be seen, then had every member of his cabinet sign it. The "blind memorandum," as it came to be known, showed that Lincoln believed his Democratic opponent in the upcoming election would be elected and would then allow the nation to dissolve.

By firing George McClellan as commanding general of the Union Army in November 1862, Lincoln made McClellan the most likely Democratic challenger for the presidency in 1864. The general had corresponded with Democratic officials since the beginning of the war; in fact, since his removal from command, party supporters had put him up in a fine house in New York

City, where his every move could be monitored by the press. McClellan strongly believed that the country should be put back together as it had been before the war started, and therefore he did not support emancipation in any way. Particularly since his forced retirement, he had publicly endorsed Democratic candidates across the North while never missing a chance to criticize Lincoln and his policies, which he believed illegally expanded the powers of the executive office. He held to the historic view that statesmen should not seek political office, but that the voters, through the parties, should seek out the individual. "I feel very indifferent about the White House," he said. "I shall do nothing to get it & trust that Providence will decide the matter as is best for the country."[14] But privately he believed that he was destined to save the country; Lincoln had ruined his opportunity to do so by leading the Army. Now he would do so by getting elected president.

The Democrats, then, felt a new surge of energy during the summer of 1864. Lincoln seemed to be particularly vulnerable. The public, they believed, could no longer abide the staggering numbers of casualties and was dissatisfied with Lincoln's policies regarding the draft and the use of black troops. Lincoln's refusal to recognize the Confederacy, and his insistence on emancipation, were impossible roadblocks on the road to peace and the restoration of the Union. Democrats believed that things were going so badly for the Republicans, in fact, that they postponed their convention from July 4 to late August, in the hope and expectation that their opponent's downward slide would continue.

The Democratic convention began in Chicago on August 29. Although the party was united in its desire to defeat Lincoln, it was far from unified on how to do it. It was divided into several factions, including the "Copperheads," or peace-at-all-costs Democrats, led by former Ohio congressman Clement Vallandigham (who had been arrested on Lincoln's order a year earlier for disloyalty); moderates who supported a limited war; and hawks who sought to win the war but disagreed with virtually all of Lincoln's policies and decisions. Ultimately the peace wing of the party successfully incorporated a proposal for a cease-fire into the official platform. Drafted by Vallandigham, the plank declared that Lincoln's "experiment" with war had been a failure and that "Justice, Humanity, Liberty and Public Welfare" required an immediate end to hostilities. But the waters then muddied for the Democrats. As expected, they chose McClellan as their candidate for president—but then nominated Congressman George Pendleton of Ohio, a peace Democrat, for vice president. Ever the military man, McClellan could not bring himself to endorse a plan for peace that recognized a Confederate nation, for that would mean that his fallen comrades had died in vain. Struggling for an identity, the party had selected candidates who disagreed with each other and endorsed a platform that its nominee would not accept.

And then, almost overnight, the war news got better for Lincoln and his party. Just days after the Democrats adjourned their convention, General Sherman announced the occupation of Atlanta, then burned the city down and began his devastating march to the coast. Then, at Mobile Bay on the Gulf of Mexico, Admiral David Farragut seized the Confederate port, his sailors spurred on by his famous order, "Damn the torpedoes, full speed ahead!" While Grant continued to lay siege to Petersburg, General Philip Sheridan finally destroyed the rebel army in the Shenandoah Valley. This series of Union successes meant assuredly that the tide was finally turning in Lincoln's favor for good.

Lincoln the politician took no chances, however; he was not above some hardball moves in the waning days of the fall campaign. He suspended habeas corpus in Kentucky from July through the elections in November, fearing, with good reason, that the region had become a breeding ground for supporters of the Southern cause. He approved treason proceedings by the military against Copperheads in Indiana, Ohio, and Pennsylvania, though there was no legal precedent to do so. He had Stanton dismiss Army quartermasters who supported McClellan or other Democrats. And he approved the practice of mandatory deductions from officers' pay, the funds diverted to the National Union Party.[15]

Lincoln also made an important move to stifle criticism in the press. He sent representatives to New York to meet with James Gordon Bennett, and then invited the newspaper editor to the White House. Lincoln offered Bennett the position of U.S. minister to France, and although Bennett ultimately turned down the offer, his criticisms of Lincoln all but disappeared in the days leading up to the election.

Lincoln believed that the election would be close and no vote could be overlooked—particularly those of loyal Union soldiers. Individual states determined how their soldiers' votes would be tabulated. Nineteen states with Republican-controlled legislatures, including Minnesota, Wisconsin, and New York, permitted their soldiers to vote in the field through absentee ballot. Illinois, Indiana, and New Jersey all had Democratic legislatures and, along with Delaware, Rhode Island, Nevada (which became a state on October 31, just before the November vote), and Oregon, did not allow field votes; soldiers from those states had to gain leave and return home to vote. Lincoln made sure that happened, for both state elections in October and the national election in November.

While Democrats perhaps assumed that many soldiers would prefer McClellan (the candidate whose party called for immediate cessation of hostilities) over Lincoln (who vowed to persist in prosecuting the war), Lincoln believed the opposite was true. He knew that he was popular with the soldiers, who called him "Father Abraham" and who had answered call after call to volunteer. Just as important, many Union soldiers wanted to continue the fight, for they did not want to believe that their efforts thus far had been in vain. They did not want to invalidate the many sacrifices of themselves or their comrades. "Uncle Abe is the soldiers' choice," said one young soldier from Iowa, summarizing the view of many soldiers. A straw poll taken at a soldiers' hospital at Annapolis resulted in 237 votes for Lincoln and just 32 for McClellan.[16]

Lincoln had always taken every opportunity to visit his soldiers in the field, to meet with them, to offer them encouragement, and to let them know how much their service was appreciated. He was particularly fond of talking with wounded veterans at the Soldiers' Home, his summer retreat in northwest Washington. Now, as the election neared, he increased his visits with soldiers and included some subtle campaigning at the same time. On August 31 he spoke to members of the 148th Ohio Regiment, who were on their way home after completing their enlistment terms. "We are striving to maintain the government and institutions of our fathers," Lincoln told them,

> to enjoy them ourselves, and transmit them to our children and our children's children forever. To the humblest and poorest amongst us are held out the highest privileges and positions. The present moment finds me at the White House, yet there is as good a chance for your children as there was for my father's son. Again I admonish you not to be turned from your stern purpose of defending your beloved country and its free institutions by any arguments urged by ambitious and designing men, but stand fast to the Union and the old flag. Soldiers, I bid you God-speed to your homes.

Soldier ballots made a difference in New York, Connecticut, Maryland, Indiana, Ohio, and Pennsylvania. In all, Lincoln received an estimated 78 percent of the soldier vote.[17]

And finally, the National Union Party relentlessly portrayed the Democrats as traitors throughout the campaign of 1864. Democrats, they charged, were far too quick to accept disunion and tolerate slavery. Worse, the so-called peace platform—"The

Great Surrender to the rebels in Arms," it was called by party spokesmen—was a knife in the back of every soldier who had fulfilled his duty and fought bravely. The men who had engineered the Democratic platform in Chicago were "the most notoriously disloyal men in the country."[18] General John Logan campaigned for Lincoln, and in a series of effective speeches he challenged voters to choose between Republican patriots who vowed to make Lincoln's "new birth of freedom" a reality, and Democratic traitors who advocated a cowardly and dishonorable peace.

On November 8, 1864, Abraham Lincoln was reelected in a landslide. He carried twenty-one states, losing only Delaware, Kentucky, and New Jersey to McClellan, with 55 percent of the popular vote. Lincoln received 212 electoral votes to only 21 for McClellan. Nineteen of twenty-three Northern states gave Lincoln more votes than they had four years earlier; his overall vote total increased by nearly 350,000 votes. Lincoln's tally proved him to be a more popular candidate than many believed, including those within his own party. And the National Union Party as a whole was successful as well. It gained seats in Congress and won governorships and state legislatures.

Lincoln took the election as a clear mandate: the war should continue until success was achieved, and success meant reunification of the Union and the elimination of slavery. Lincoln's reelection shattered morale in the South. It proved that it was not only Lincoln's resolve to persevere, but the resolve of the Northern public as well. The people had spoken, loudly and firmly, and the principles of reunion and emancipation would triumph.

Although Jefferson Davis remained defiant, at least outwardly, and vowed that the Confederacy would never capitulate, the election would help the Union win the war. Ulysses S. Grant predicted as much. "The overwhelming majority received by Mr. Lincoln, and the quiet with which the election went off, will provide a terrible damper to the rebels," he said. "It will be worth more than a victory in the field both in its effects on the rebels and in its influence abroad." Lincoln agreed, saying, "We cannot have free government without elections, and if the rebellion could force us to forgo or postpone a national election, it might fairly claim to have already conquered and ruined us." Lincoln's reelection was much more than a political triumph for a person, or a party. Coming as it did in the midst of a great civil war, it was a victory for the Union.

7

Rising Above the Fray:
Second Term

If the end brings me out all right, what is said against me won't amount to anything. If the end brings me out wrong, ten angels swearing I was right would make no difference.

—Abraham Lincoln, White House conversation, 1865

His reelection handily won, Lincoln was hopeful that his second term would be marked by peace, progress, and prosperity instead of war and discontent. Though the events of 1864 had left him exhausted, Lincoln had neither the time nor the inclination to rest. He kept up a staggering workload in the fall and winter, reviewing requests for pardons and results of courts-martial, attending cabinet meetings, huddling with congressional delegations, and attending public levees and functions. Just as after his election in 1860, he was hounded by office seekers, and once again he met with as many applicants as possible, and tried to reward as many of the party faithful as he could. Mary noticed the physical toll that presidential duties and the sadness of the war continued to take on her husband. "Mr. Lincoln is so broken hearted, so completely worn out," she fretted.[1] But there was still much left to do, and his second term had not even begun.

Lincoln first had to deal with the makeup of his cabinet. As is the case with any two-term president, it was widely speculated that Lincoln would replace some or all of his top advisers. But some of the problems that had plagued and disrupted the group in his first term had been taken care of in recent months. The self-righteous and overtly ambitious Salmon Chase had resigned as secretary of the Treasury in June, replaced by the radical Senator William Fessenden of Maine. Postmaster General Montgomery Blair, the enemy of the radicals, had left in the wake of John C. Frémont's presidential bid and been replaced by William Dennison of Ohio. Much of the bickering that had hampered the cabinet in the first term had now ceased, and Lincoln was satisfied that the newly formed group worked well together and, with some relatively minor tinkering, would continue to do so.

The president particularly enjoyed the respectful relationship he had forged with Secretary of State William Seward, with whom he conferred daily. Seward had the president's ear on the most important matters and gave thoughtful, reasoned advice. He came to realize that Lincoln controlled his cabinet and not the reverse, and fully accepted that fact. He assured his leader and friend that his own presidential aspirations had abated, and he worked hard for the president's reelection. Seward thought that Lincoln "should be his own successor," and when that occurred "the rebellion will collapse."[2] As he grew more comfortable in his role as chief confidant of the president, Seward's admiration for Lincoln's resolve grew stronger. "Lincoln will take his place with Washington and Franklin, and Jefferson, and Adams, and Jackson, among the benefactors of the country and of the human race," Seward said after his chief's reelection.[3] Lincoln thought highly of Seward as well. The friendship between the two men was "absolute and sincere," wrote Lincoln's secretary John Hay. "No shadow of jealousy or doubt ever disturbed their mutual confidence and regard."[4]

The president was less friendly with his secretary of war, Edwin Stanton, but the two men had managed to forge an effective working relationship. Periodically bedridden, Stanton refused doctor's orders for extended rest, usually working fifteen-hour days (almost never sitting down, but preferring to direct operations from his stand-up desk), instructing his physician to "keep me alive till this rebellion is over."[5] Perhaps the greatest tension between the two men arose because of Lincoln's inclination to grant pardons in liberal fashion, even for such seemingly inexcusable offenses as desertion or dereliction of duty. Lincoln always looked for an excuse to spare a soldier's life, particularly when the man's wife or mother intervened. Stanton the disciplinarian felt compelled to keep military discipline, and believed that sure and swift punishment acted as a powerful deterrent to possible offenders. Serious and stubborn, often abrasively honest, Stanton regularly gave Lincoln advice in his blunt, gruff manner, which the president received while understanding that Stanton's pressure-packed job "is one of the most difficult in the world."[6] Next to Lincoln, Stanton received more public criticism than anyone, his every movement, order, and decision scrutinized and debated. But his chief was quick to defend Stanton's performance. "Folks come up here and tell me that there are a great many men in the country who have all Stanton's excellent qualities without his defects," he said. "All I have to say is, I haven't met 'em! I don't know 'em!"[7]

Lincoln was equally pleased with the work of Secretary of the Navy Gideon Welles. Welles, to be sure, often disagreed with the president on policy matters—for example, he opposed the suspension of the writ of habeas corpus and was fearful that the Emancipation Proclamation would fuel the Southern war effort and lengthen the war. But Welles kept his criticisms private, sharing his feelings only in the diary he faithfully kept. Driven by a strong sense of duty, he was faithful to the president, serving as a go-between when Lincoln and Chase argued and discreetly trying to restore working order to the cabinet. While initially distrustful of Lincoln's scheme to blockade Southern ports, Welles had vigorously enforced the plan with a fleet that he had built into a world-class power. Under Welles's direction the American Navy had grown from 76 vessels to 671, and the number of seamen from 7,600 to 51,000.

John Usher had been secretary of the interior since 1862, when he had succeeded Caleb Smith, who became a federal judge. Usher was the least controversial cabinet member. He went about his job dutifully, with little fanfare. He was loyal to the president and rarely offered his opinions at cabinet meetings; for his part Lincoln seems seldom to have sought Usher's advice. One notable exception concerned the Minnesota Sioux Indian uprising of 1862. Bands of starving Sioux, upset over years of mistreatment by corrupt government agents, revolted and killed hundreds of prairie homesteaders. General John Pope, so ineffective against Confederate forces in Virginia, was sent to Minnesota to put down the rebellion. Amid growing clamor from outraged whites, Pope proclaimed that he meant to "exterminate the Sioux." The number of Indians killed by federal soldiers is unknown, but nearly fifteen hundred were arrested and summarily convicted by military tribunal. More than three hundred were sentenced to death, and Lincoln felt pressure from Minnesota politicians to approve the executions. Usher went to Minnesota to investigate the situation, then returned to Washington and discussed with Lincoln the jurisdictional and procedural problems raised by the actions of the tribunal. Acting partly upon Usher's advice, Lincoln insisted on reviewing, individually, the records of the convicted participants. He finally approved the execution of thirty-eight men who were guilty of murder or rape. The case proved to be Usher's only noteworthy achievement, however, and by the spring of 1865 Lincoln would replace him with Senator James Harlan of Iowa (who would become the father-in-law of the president's son Robert Todd Lincoln).

That left Edward Bates as attorney general. Now seventy-one years of age, Bates had been a loyal supporter of Lincoln and had served with distinction. A strong advocate of the president's war powers authority, Bates had written legal opinions justifying the suspension of habeas corpus and the Emancipation Proclamation. A critic of the *Dred Scott* decision, Bates championed combat duty for black soldiers as well as equal pay for equal service. But now that the election had been won, Bates was urged by his family to return to his home in St. Louis, and Lincoln accepted his resignation cordially. In his place the president sought to nominate Joseph Holt, Judge Advocate General of the Army, but Holt declined. Lincoln then chose the man Holt suggested: Kentucky lawyer James Speed, the brother of his old friend Joshua Speed. Speed had worked for Lincoln's reelection, declaring himself a "Constitutional Abolitionist," which meant that, like Lincoln, he was "for abolishing Slavery under the War Power of the National Constitution, and then clinching it by a Constitutional amendment prohibiting it everywhere forever."[8]

In all, then, Lincoln was pleased with the makeup of his second cabinet, and hopeful that it would prove to be an effective group. Unlike the original cabinet of four years earlier, only Seward was a significant leader within the Republican Party. No one questioned Lincoln's character, his intelligence, or his abilities. No one had any aspirations to be president; in fact, all felt deep personal loyalty to Lincoln. The group was balanced politically; with the addition of Dennison and Speed, even the radicals were satisfied for the time being. Most important, the group pledged to work together in furtherance of Lincoln's policies in the second term of his administration.

Lincoln had made significant changes to the Supreme Court during his first term, appointing four new justices to the bench. He made an even more important move in October 1864 when Chief Justice Roger Taney died. The ancient Maryland native and slaveholder had written the infamous *Dred Scott* decision, declaring that "black people had no rights which the white man was bound to respect," and had been very critical of the legality of

Lincoln's war policies throughout the war. Now Lincoln had the opportunity to replace Taney with a man more sympathetic to moderate Republican views, which was particularly important in view of his forthcoming plans for reconstruction. As always, Lincoln balanced practicality and politics in choosing his nominee. Not surprisingly, the names of men who had served in his cabinet came to the fore: Stanton, Blair, Bates, and Chase. Lincoln struggled with his decision, took advice from many friends, politicians and otherwise, and finally selected Chase. Lincoln had long been weary of Chase's pettiness and scheming but could not help but admire his abilities. "We have stood together in the time of trial," he said, "and I should despise myself if I allowed personal differences to affect my judgment of his fitness for the office. . . . His only trouble is that he has 'the White House fever' a little too bad, but I hope this may cure him and that he will be satisfied."[9] Again, the radicals within the Republican Party would be satisfied with his choice. Now, along with his other appointees, Lincoln could rest assured that the Supreme Court would look disfavorably upon any challenges to his actions and policies—and would be inclined to respect the rights of African Americans. Within months, Lincoln's hopes began to be at least partially realized: in January, Chief Justice Chase approved the admission of John Rock of Massachusetts, making him the first black man to practice before the Supreme Court.

As he prepared to deliver his annual message to Congress in December, Lincoln reflected on the legislative achievements of his first term, which had been all but overlooked because of the country's preoccupation with the war. Many new laws, passed by the Republican-controlled Congress, would prove to have long-lasting consequences as the nation pushed relentlessly westward, settling new lands and expanding its borders.

A series of financial measures had been enacted to fund the war, which was costing $2 million daily. Under the direction of the Treasury Department, and with the administrative guidance of the Philadelphia banker Jay Cooke, the government had issued war bonds (which, over the course of the war, would raise about $3 billion for the Union, or 65 percent of its revenue). Needing an unrestricted currency supply to fuel the bond program, Congress passed the Legal Tender Act in 1862, which authorized the production and distribution of paper money, known popularly as greenbacks.

More significantly, the Internal Revenue Act of 1861, the first federal income tax in American history, assured the financial community that the government would have a reliable source of income to pay the interest on war bonds. Subsequent Revenue Acts of 1862 and 1864 created moderately progressive tax brackets and set rates at 5, 7.5, and 10 percent. By the end of the war nearly one in ten American households (mostly in the affluent states in the industrial Northeast, the section of the country that held most of the wealth) paid an income tax.

Also enacted was an excise tax system that imposed taxes on almost everything: liquor, professional licenses, carriages, yachts, medicines, corporations, stamps, and the like. The Morrill Tariff Acts of 1860 and 1861 doubled the amounts of taxes collected on dutiable items brought into the United States, while at the same time protecting the steel, iron, mineral, beef, and fishing industries, among many others. Congress also enacted the National Banking Acts of 1863 and 1864, which established a system of national charters for banks and encouraged the implementation of a national currency. They also mandated that one-third of a new bank's notes had to be backed by federal bonds, thus assisting the war effort. When state banks balked at the new regulation, a provision of the 1864 Act imposed a 10 percent tax on state bank notes; state banks then had to choose to comply or go out of business. Overall, the tax system quickly grew so large that the Bureau of Internal Revenue was created to administer it.

These finance measures reversed the downward trends instituted by Democratic Congresses of the 1840s and 1850s, and fulfilled Republican promises from the campaign of 1860.

During Lincoln's first term, the Republican Congress also passed the Homestead Act of 1862, which made public lands in the West available for small farmers. For decades the distribution of these lands had been the subject of great debate and controversy, in Washington and among the American population. Under the new Homestead Act, any adult citizen who headed a household could win title to 160 acres of frontier land simply by living on it for five years. By the end of the war more than fifteen thousand homestead claims had been filed, with more to come. While some portion of the land ended up in the control of speculators and railroads, many settlers stuck it out, raised their families, and harvested crops, thereby establishing a framework for the large-scale development of vast Western territories over the course of the next forty years. The 160-acre tracts created the model of the American family farm for the next century.

Also in 1862 Lincoln signed into law the Morrill Land Grant College Act, named for Senator Justin Morrill of Vermont. The statute transferred federal lands to states to be sold for the establishment and support of agricultural and mechanical arts colleges, which paved the way for the establishment of state university systems throughout the Midwest and West. The program was set up proportionately, dependent upon the number of congressional representatives, and eventually involved the transfer of nearly seventeen million acres of land. That same year, Congress and Lincoln established the Department of Agriculture to look after the interests of farmers (although the department would not gain cabinet-level status for some twenty years).

These three landmark acts—the Homestead Act, the Land Grant College Act, and the creation of the U.S. Department of Agriculture, all enacted in the middle of the Civil War—formed a tripod on which much of America's great agricultural success has rested from that day until the present.

Also of great importance was the passage of the Pacific Railway Acts of 1862 and 1864. These laws provided for the construction of a railroad and telegraph line from Omaha to Sacramento for the movement of passengers and freight as well as government use for postal, military, and other purposes. All told, the Union Pacific and Central Pacific railroads received more than 175 million acres from the government for use as right-of-way, and began construction. Utilizing thousands of immigrant laborers from Ireland, Germany, Italy, and China, and with the Union Pacific pushing west and the Central Pacific pushing east, the two lines met and merged near Ogden, Utah, in 1869, finally and forever linking the two coasts. Lincoln's support for all these laws was a reflection of the Whig principles that had nurtured him: the belief that the federal government could and should play an important role in the public welfare.

Reconstruction of the Union had been on Lincoln's mind since the important battlefield victories of 1863. At some point, he believed, the erring rebel states would have to be taken back and the country restored. But on what terms? Lincoln never considered secession to be legal, and he never acknowledged the existence of the Confederacy or the legitimacy of Jefferson Davis's presidency. He felt that many Southerners—perhaps a majority—had been misled into believing that the only way to protect their way of life from destruction by Lincoln was by secession and war. Lincoln, therefore, wanted reconstruction to take place gently, with a measure of forgiveness. He was not out to punish the Confederates; he did, however, want reunification to be accomplished quickly. Convinced that reconstruction was a province of the executive office and of individual states (not of Congress), in December 1863 he issued a Proclamation of Amnesty and Reconstruction, aimed at Southern areas occupied by federal forces. Lincoln hoped that the generous terms of the proclamation would entice war-weary Southern soldiers to lay down their arms while building popular (and political) support in the North.

Lincoln's proposal came to be called the Ten Percent Plan: that is, once 10 percent of a state's citizens swore an oath of allegiance to the national government, the state could be readmitted to the Union. Those citizens (excluding high-ranking Confederate officers and government officials) would be granted a full pardon. Elected delegates would then draft new state constitutions (explicitly abolishing slavery) and reestablish state governments. Once those simple conditions were met, Lincoln would offer an "executive recognition" of the state. Moderate Republicans endorsed Lincoln's plan, believing that the surest way to end the war was to extend an olive branch. But the always vocal radical Republicans vilified it. Insisting that reconstruction was solely a legislative function, they wanted to punish the rebels for causing hundreds of thousands of deaths in an unnecessary war. Radicals meant to reformulate Southern society by guaranteeing civil liberties for blacks. They feared that Lincoln's overly lenient plan would simply reestablish the old planter aristocracy, when instead that old order, which had in fact caused the war, needed to be replaced with a more modern, industrial-based economic system.

With these objectives in mind, the radicals managed to push the more stringent Wade-Davis bill through Congress in the summer of 1864, as discussed in chapter 6. The bill required that 50 percent of a state's voters take an "ironclad" oath renouncing the Confederacy and supporting the Union before the state could qualify for readmission. Further, the bill would outlaw slave ownership, making it a federal crime punishable by imprisonment and fine. The president would appoint, and the Senate would confirm, provisional governors who would call a constitutional convention and reorganize the state government. Once approved by Congress, the state could hold state and federal elections, making the reconstruction process complete. Lincoln vetoed the bill, insisting that since Congress had no power to interfere with slavery, it also had no power to abolish slavery through a reconstruction measure. With the president and Congress now at odds over how and when reconstruction might occur, the issue would have to wait.

. . .

Lincoln's annual message to Congress, which he delivered on December 6, 1864, summarized his thoughts and feelings on a number of important topics as he looked to his second term. First addressing foreign affairs, he told Congress that the state of America's relations with Mexico, Russia, China, and many other countries was "reasonably satisfactory." Next Lincoln dealt with financial matters. "The financial affairs of the Government have been successfully administered during the last year," he said. The Treasury showed a balance of almost nineteen million dollars, but additional taxes needed to be levied to meet the expected war expenses. Quickly summarizing domestic affairs, Lincoln spoke of the building of the transcontinental railroad, the conversion to a national banking system, and the need to reorganize and remodel government bureaucracies to "improve the condition of the Indian."

"The war continues," Lincoln said. Union armies had steadily advanced—he noted Sherman's relentless march through the heart of the South—and there was reason to be optimistic about the future. Lincoln's will to maintain the integrity of the national government remained strong. The American people had demonstrated a like commitment over the four long years of war; America's people, in fact, remained its greatest asset. And while the nation surely mourned the hundreds of thousands dead, "we do not approach exhaustion" in terms of living men. Many more were available to fight and, more important, willing to fight for their country.

Without mentioning Jefferson Davis by name, Lincoln insisted that he would never recognize the rebel government and hinted that its leader was out of touch with those he led. "No attempt at negotiation with an insurgent leader could result in any good," he said.

> He cannot voluntarily reaccept the Union; we can not voluntarily yield it. . . . It is an issue which can only be tried by war and decided by victory. . . . What is true, however, of him who heads the insurgent cause is not necessarily true of those who follow. Although he can not reaccept the Union, they can. Some of them, we know, already desire peace and reunion. . . . They can at any moment have peace simply by laying down their arms and submitting to that national authority under the Constitution. . . . In stating a single condition of peace I mean simply to say that the war will cease on the part of the Government whenever it shall have ceased on the part of those who began it.[10]

Slavery had divided the country and brought on the war. Lincoln now addressed the issue and defended his policies: "I retract nothing heretofore said as to slavery. I repeat the declaration made a year ago, that 'while I remain in my present position I shall not attempt to retract or modify the emancipation proclamation, nor shall I return to slavery any person who is free by the terms of that proclamation or by any of the acts of Congress.' "

Lincoln dearly wanted to permanently abolish slavery through constitutional amendment. Undoubtedly he was concerned that his Emancipation Proclamation would be revoked once the war was over. While the Supreme Court, with its newer members, would in all likelihood uphold the proclamation as legally valid, there was no way of knowing for certain. The proclamation—issued as a military necessity—had been limited in scope, freeing only those slaves in rebel states. Lincoln was worried that a judicial decision might also be limited, and that it perhaps might ratify freedom of only those former slaves who "came into our lines . . . or that it would have no effect upon the children of the slaves born hereafter." Passage of a constitutional amendment would solve these problems for all time, "a King's cure for all the evils," Lincoln phrased it.[11]

Why should this lame-duck Congress vote to pass the amendment? Lincoln believed that the American people had spoken loudly in the election. The Republican Party, at Lincoln's insistence, had supported the amendment in its platform. The party had won the election by overwhelming numbers; surely, then, the next Congress would pass the necessary legislation. He had the option of calling a special session after his second inauguration on March 4, but he wanted to avoid that step. "May we not agree that the sooner the better?" asked Lincoln.

The Constitution had not been amended in sixty years. The first ten amendments, or Bill of Rights, were drafted by James Madison and had been adopted in 1791. The Eleventh Amendment, ratified in 1795, clarified judicial power and the sovereign immunity of states. And the Twelfth Amendment, which concerned the Electoral College, was added to the Constitution in 1804. John Quincy Adams had proposed an amendment to abolish slavery in 1839, but it gained very little support.

Even with eleven Southern states still out of the Union in 1864 and thus unable to vote on the measure, a constitutional amendment was not an easy undertaking. In 1863 two Republican congressmen, James Ashley of Ohio and James Wilson of Iowa, had introduced a bill to support an amendment, but it failed. So did similar proposals by the war Democrat John Henderson of Missouri and the Radical Republican Charles Sumner of Massachusetts. (One part of Sumner's plan guaranteed equality and civil rights for blacks, probably dooming its chances.) One year later the Senate Judiciary Committee, under the leadership of Lyman Trumbull, submitted a bill that combined various proposals, and the measure passed the Senate in April by a vote of 38 to 6. It failed to pass the House, and further talk of a constitutional amendment quieted. Now was the time, argued Lincoln, for Congress to reconsider. At Lincoln's urging, Congressman Ashley reintroduced his measure in January 1865, utilizing simple and direct language: "Neither slavery nor involuntary servitude, except as a punishment for a crime whereof the party shall have been duly convicted, shall exist within the United States, nor any place subject to their jurisdiction." Further, "Congress shall have power to enforce this article by appropriate legislation." This language seems to make clear that Congress plays a key role in any move to terminate slavery. An amendment would not have the teeth needed to end slavery without a plan and enforcement methods to carry it into operation.

But opposition to the amendment remained formidable. Democratic congressman George Pendleton of Ohio, who had been George McClellan's running mate for vice president, led the fight. Pendleton had been a vocal critic of Lincoln's suspension of habeas corpus and his other civil rights policies, and now, as a politician of some clout in Washington, he advised his fellow Democrats that they faced dire consequences if they failed to follow the party line and voted for the amendment. The amendment, he warned his colleagues, would mark a severe blow to states' rights.

Lincoln used his talents as a master politician to work tirelessly to gain the necessary votes. According to the historian Michael Vorenberg, "No piece of legislation during Lincoln's presidency received more of his attention than the Thirteenth Amendment."[12] He knew he had to persuade conservative Republicans, border-state Unionists, and (particularly) moderate Democrats to support the amendment, and he invited many of them to the White House for private conversations. One former Whig, James Rollins of Missouri, was told that his vote for the amendment could help end the war by showing that the border states could no longer be relied upon to support slavery. Lincoln invoked the name of Henry Clay, who undoubtedly would have supported the measure. The vote, said Lincoln, "was going to be very close, a few votes one way or the other will decide it." Could he count on Rollins's support? When he received that assurance, Lincoln took hold of Rollins's hands and shook them with gratitude. Tell the other Missouri congressmen of your decision, Lincoln told Rollins. "Tell them of my anxiety to have the measure pass and let me know the prospect of the border state vote."

Lincoln offered federal jobs to congressmen (or their family members) of both parties in exchange for votes. He twisted arms and called in favors. Politicians whose seats were seen as tenuous were promised support. One congressman, an attorney for a railroad that faced adverse legislation, was assured of political cooperation. Democrat Moses Odell of Brooklyn, for example, was promised, and received, the post of Navy agent in New York, a highly sought-after position. Lincoln assigned politicos to gain the votes of two uncertain House members, telling them that "the abolition of slavery by constitutional provision settles the fate, for all coming time, not only of the millions now in bondage, but of unborn millions to come—a measure of such importance that *those two votes must be procured*. I leave it to you to determine how it shall be done; but remember that I am President of the United States, clothed with immense power, and I expect you to procure those votes." And Lincoln was pleased when his words were quoted—"If slavery is not wrong, nothing is wrong"—on the floor of the House.

The measure came up for final debate and vote in the House on January 31, 1865. The gallery was jammed to capacity with newspapermen, congressional staffers, family members, and other observers. Others stood in the lobby outside the chamber, while hundreds more were turned away. Many senators had to search for a vacant chair on the House floor, along with foreign dignitaries, cabinet members, and justices of the Supreme Court. Rumors circulated that Confederate peace commissioners had arrived in Washington; if that were true, some Democrats, believing peace was at hand, might not support the amendment. Lincoln wrote to James Ashley, "So far as I know, there are no peace commissioners in the city, or likely to be in it." The message was purposely misleading, for Lincoln knew that three peace representatives were just a few miles away, at Fort Monroe. Lincoln's cunning, Ashley believed, probably saved the bill.

Debate began at ten o'clock in the morning. Ashley believed that passage of the amendment represented all he had worked for in his political life; still, he wisely yielded his time in favor of Democrats who needed to publicly justify their switch in votes. Archibald McAllister of Pennsylvania explained that his aye vote signified a vote for peace, for the amendment would "destroy the corner-stone of the Southern Confederacy."[13] His comments, as well as similar comments from his fellow Democrats, were met with cheers.

At four o'clock, Speaker of the House Schuyler Colfax announced the tally of the vote: the measure passed by a vote of 119 to 58, with 8 abstaining—just three votes more than the required two-thirds majority. The gallery erupted in shouting and whistles, "a storm of cheers, the likes of which probably no Congress of the United States ever heard before."[14] Normally staid congressmen stood and applauded. By the prearranged order of Edwin Stanton, a hundred-gun cannon salute rocked the city of Washington. Of those who had voted in favor, and particularly those five Democrats who had changed their vote, Stanton said, "History will embalm them in great honor."[15] Congressman George Julian of Indiana wrote in his diary, "I have felt, ever since the vote, as if I were in a new country."[16]

The abolitionist William Lloyd Garrison, who had often criticized Lincoln for his slow pace in working toward emancipation, now praised him as the "chainbreaker for millions of the oppressed," and acknowledged that the amendment would never have passed without Lincoln's skillful guidance.[17] At a celebration at the White House, Lincoln told a group of admirers that the matter was "a great moral victory. . . . The occasion was one of congratulation to the country and to the whole world."[18] Privately he told aides that the amendment consummated his "own great work," the Emancipation Proclamation.

Unwilling to take any chances, Lincoln floated a plan to pay some $400 million to the states in exchange for ratification of the amendment. The cabinet unanimously rejected the idea as unnecessary, and Lincoln discarded it. Quickly he learned that there was no need for payments: within the year the required three-quarters of states had ratified the Thirteenth Amendment, ending slavery in America forever. And the very first state to do so, Lincoln proudly noted, was Illinois.

8

Victory and Death

Now he belongs to the Ages.
—Edwin Stanton, April 15, 1865

It had been four painful, catastrophic years for America. Both sides had thought the war would be over quickly, but it had dragged on so long that the numbers reached staggering, unimaginable levels. More than ten thousand battles had been fought in sixteen states, plus the New Mexico and Indian territories. Of the three million men who took up arms against each other, more than six hundred thousand had died; two-thirds of those deaths were by disease. Many thousands of soldiers, North and South, went home without a leg or an arm, a face, testicles, eyes, or feet. Others went home with permanently damaged brains or nervous systems. More than 150 prisons were established to house prisoners of war; all were quickly filled to capacity, and more than fifty thousand men died in them from disease, exposure, and malnutrition. Conditions in the prisons on both sides were disgraceful, morally outrageous. Half-crazed prisoners frequently beat or killed one another while fighting for near-starvation food rations. On the brighter side, some four million African American slaves had been set free, and when finally given the chance 185,000 fought bravely for the Union that they hoped might somehow fulfill its promises of liberty and justice.

The grim figure of six hundred thousand for those who died in the Civil War is only slightly below the combined American fatalities in the two world wars. These terrible losses came at a time when the U.S. population was much smaller than it was during the world wars. Nearly every family across the land, North and South, lost a son, a husband, a brother, a cousin, an uncle, or a friend or neighbor. Of course, this war set an all-time record for American fatalities because the people who died on both sides were all Americans.

Wheatfields and cornfields became killing grounds. Churches became hospitals, homes became military headquarters. From the Atlantic Ocean to the Mississippi River, American waterways were streaked with blood. Armies pursued each other, seeking to destroy not only enemy soldiers but transportation lines, factories, towns, and farms. The federal government looked to defeat the Confederate army in the field and to break the will of the Southern people. In response, the rebels struggled so desperately to survive that their government forced nearly every available male to fight. Both sides fought savagely, heroically, relentlessly. But the exuberant fanfare of 1861, manifested in parades and celebrations and patriotic fever—the sense of adventure that so many thousands of young men felt as they went off to war—had been replaced by a grim weariness and sober realization of the horrors that had been inflicted. Both sides suffered from a shattered spirit. "The immense slaughter of our brave men chills and sickens us all," said Gideon Welles.[1] By 1865 Robert E. Lee realized that the longer the war went on, the less chance the Confederates had of winning it. Lincoln and Grant understood this inescapable fact as well.

The war had taken a heavy personal toll on Lincoln. Four years of bloodshed and destruction haunted and drained him. He slept and ate poorly. His clothes hung comically on his gaunt frame. "I am very unwell," Lincoln said. "My feet and hands are always cold—I suppose I should be in bed."[2] Orville Browning, Lincoln's friend and critic from Illinois, visited him in February and found him "more depressed than I have seen him since he became President."[3] Photographs of the fifty-six-year-old Lincoln show him sad-eyed and careworn with the unmistakable look of exhaustion. Even his famed sense of humor did not surface as often; "the boisterous laughter became less frequent year by year," said his secretary John Hay.[4] "I am a tired man," Lincoln said. "Sometimes I think I am the tiredest man on earth."[5]

Once during the war when a delegation of women were waiting to see the president at the White House they heard him laughing. When they were admitted to his office, the leader of the delegation told Lincoln that they were dismayed to hear the president laughing while American boys were dying on the battlefield. Lincoln is reported to have replied that if it were not for occasional laughter to break his sadness over the war his heart would break.

Still, remarkably, Lincoln willed himself to carry on. As weakened as he was physically, his spirit, buoyed by an inner strength, remained strong. Since his election in 1860 he had seemingly experienced a deepening of his faith. The death of his favorite son, Willie, in 1862 devastated him and Mary, but he took to heart the advice of a Presbyterian minister who told him to turn to God with confidence, for "our sorrows will be sanctified and made a blessing to our souls, and by and by we shall have occasion to say with blended gratitude and rejoicing, 'It is good for us that we have been afflicted.' " He came to acknowledge, and even depend upon, a higher power; indeed, it seemed that the connection between Lincoln and the Almighty enabled him to take on the great challenges he faced as president. He saw himself as an instrument of God's will; he had been charged with a "vast" and "sacred" trust, the responsibilities from which he "had no moral right to shrink." Still, Lincoln did not expect that God would show him the way. "These are not . . . the days of miracles," he said. "I must study the plain physical facts of the case, ascertain what is possible and learn what appears to be wise and right." He had to trust his own judgment as well as God's. "In the present civil war," he wrote, "it is quite possible that God's purpose is something different from the purpose of either party. . . . He could give the final victory to either side any day—yet the contest proceeds."[6]

For all his trials, Lincoln had become a masterful president. His political skills and powers of persuasion were unmatched. His self-confidence was strong, and he demonstrated great faith in his abilities and in the worthiness of his cause. The depth of his insight, and his ability to judge and inspire men, had transformed him into an extraordinary leader. Lincoln's growth was unexpected, certainly, to most who knew him. But he had guided—and was guiding—the nation through unprecedented times, and he had a vision for the future.

Lincoln summoned all his skills as he prepared for his second Inauguration Day. Saturday, March 4, 1865, broke cold and wet in Washington. Despite the weather a large crowd assembled in front of the East Portico of the Capitol. Just as Lincoln moved to the lectern the sun emerged from the clouds, bathing the speaking stand in glorious light. He hesitated a few moments, taking in the sustained applause, and then spoke in his high, clear voice. Memorable and magnificent, the speech was notable for both its content and its literary style. Lincoln did not dwell on the achievements of his presidency, did not even mention the Emancipation Proclamation. He gave no hint that Union forces were on the road to certain victory. Instead, he sought to explain the origin of the conflict and examine its significance. He spoke of Providence, and the idea of exact retribution: God might punish the nation for the sin of slavery, he believed, the North for allowing the evil institution to exist, and the South for the institution itself. Most famously, Lincoln spoke of the need for mutual forgiveness and the promise of a reunited America.

Four years earlier, Lincoln said, "all thoughts were anxiously directed to an impending civil war." Both sides "deprecated war; but one of them would *make* war rather than let the nation survive; and the other would *accept* war rather than let it perish. And the war came." One-eighth of the American population, Lincoln noted, were slaves, "who constituted a peculiar and powerful interest. All knew this interest was, somehow, the cause of the war."

Many on both North and South claimed that God was on their side, continued Lincoln. "Both read the same Bible, and pray to the same God. And each invokes His aid against the other. . . . The prayers of both could not be answered; that of neither has been answered fully. The Almighty has his own purposes." Those purposes would surely be revealed in the months to come, Lincoln cautioned:

> Fondly do we hope—fervently do we pray—that this mighty scourge of war may speedily pass away. Yet, if God wills that it continue, until all the wealth piled by the bond-man's two hundred and fifty years of unrequited toil shall be sunk, and until every drop of blood drawn with the lash, shall be paid by another drawn with the sword, as was said three thousand years ago, so still it must be said "the judgments of the Lord, are true and righteous altogether."

Lincoln concluded with the immortal peroration of forgiveness, reconciliation, and healing: "With malice toward none; with charity for all; with firmness in the right, as God gives us to see the right, let us strive on to finish the work we are in; to bind up the nation's wounds; to care for him who shall have borne the battle, and for his widow, and his orphan—to do all which may achieve and cherish a just and lasting peace, among ourselves, and with all nations."[7]

At just 703 words, Lincoln's second inaugural address was the shortest in American history. It was met with mixed reviews, but

Lincoln was not nearly as concerned with press reaction as he once had been. He was more pleased when Frederick Douglass, in attendance at a White House reception that evening, told him the speech was a "sacred effort."[8] Lincoln believed that the speech might "wear as well—perhaps better than—any thing I have produced; but I believe it is not immediately popular. Men are not flattered by being shown that there has been a difference of purpose between the Almighty and them. It is a truth which I thought needed to be told."[9]

Another truth was that the end of the war was in sight. General Sherman's mighty and relentless march continued through the winter. He had reached Savannah at Christmas, and then turned his destructive machine north into South Carolina. "The devil himself couldn't restrain my men," said Sherman. "I almost tremble at her [the South's] fate, but feel that she deserves all that seems to be in store for her."[10] Charleston fell in mid-February, and Sherman set his sights on the rear of Lee's faltering Army of Virginia.

Since June 1864, Lee had been rendered immobile at Petersburg, just a few miles south of the capital city of Richmond. The junction point of five railroads, Petersburg was the Confederacy's essential supply center, and Grant knew that if he could take it, he could take Richmond itself. The federals matched rebel fortifications with trench lines that extended for thirty miles along its southern and eastern perimeters. For ten months Grant had launched a series of assaults on the city but had been met with stubborn, if ever-weakening, resistance on all fronts. Eventually, Grant believed, Lee's line of defense would be stretched so thin that it would break.

Grant invited the Lincolns to Union headquarters at City Point, Virginia, just ten miles northeast of Petersburg. On March 23, Lincoln and Mary, her maid, twelve-year-old Tad, and two guards boarded the *River Queen* and sailed down the Potomac, while Edwin Stanton, concerned for Lincoln's safety, remained anxiously in Washington. For the first time in weeks Lincoln was able to relax, and he thoroughly enjoyed the trip, exploring the ship, talking with the crew, and taking in the scenery. Mary later recalled that the pleasant river excursion, combined with Lincoln's hope that "the war was near its close," put him in a cheerful mood. "He was almost boyish, in his mirth & reminded me, of his original nature, what I had always remembered of him, in our own home—free from care, surrounded by those he loved so well."[11] Captain Robert Lincoln—until recently a student at Harvard, and now, upon his father's special request, a member of Grant's staff— escorted General and Mrs. Grant to greet the Lincolns when the *River Queen* docked at City Point on the evening of March 24. While the women chatted, Grant reassured his president that the war was indeed winding down.

The next morning, however, brought surprising news. Nearly half of Lee's army, under General John Gordon, had broken away from the Petersburg lines and attacked Fort Stedman, just eight miles away. It appeared that Lee's plan was to move his army to North Carolina and join forces with Joe Johnston; together, perhaps, Lee and Johnston could block Sherman from joining Grant, and the rebel war effort might survive. But Grant's forces under George Meade and John Parke moved quickly to check Gordon, inflicting nearly three thousand casualties on the Confederate army.

Lincoln was eager to view the battlefield and telegraphed Stanton that he was "here within five miles of this morning's action." A special train was organized, and Lincoln rode over military rail to Stedman and General Meade's headquarters. Lincoln toured the field on horseback, seeing fresh evidence of the most recent carnage: the ground covered with dead and wounded men of both sides, surgeons attending to soldiers in the field while ambulances carried others away to hospitals, and burial parties already at work. Lincoln remarked "upon the sad and unhappy condition" of long lines of Confederate prisoners, most of whom appeared undernourished and resigned to defeat. Later he said that "he had seen enough of the horrors of war, and that he hoped this would be the beginning of the end, and that there would be no more bloodshed or ruin of homes."[12] His train returned slowly to City Point, and Lincoln, depressed over what he had seen, canceled his plans for dinner with Grant, preferring to spend time alone with Mary.

Lincoln remained at City Point for the next several days, conferring with commanders, discussing strategy, and studying the constant stream of telegraph dispatches. He spent a considerable amount of time at the local hospital, visiting thousands of wounded Union and Confederate soldiers. One observer, an employee with the United States Sanitary Commission, said that when talking to rebels "he was just as kind, his handshakings just as hearty, his interest just as real for the welfare of the men, as when he was among our own soldiers."[13] On March 26 he reviewed General Ord's division at Malvern Hill. Mary arrived late, and she saw Mrs. Ord riding close to Lincoln, a position of honor that she believed should have been reserved for herself. She exploded in anger, calling Mrs. Ord "vile names," much to the embarrassment of everyone present. Her angry mood continued that evening at dinner, despite Lincoln's gentle reassurances that no slight had been intended, and she finally retreated to her stateroom, where she remained secluded for several days. Much to Lincoln's relief, Mary made plans to return to Washington on April 1.

Fresh from a victory over Johnston at Bentonville, North Carolina, and with his army resupplying at Goldsboro, General Sherman arrived at City Point to confer with Lincoln and Grant. The three men, along with Admiral David Dixon Porter, met on board the *River Queen* and entered into "a lively conversation" about the military situation and how best to corner Lee and bring about the end of the conflict. Both generals agreed that Lee's only option, short of releasing his men to fight as guerrillas, was to fall back in desperation to the Carolinas. Lee had been trapped before, only to outmaneuver his opponent and escape. It must not be allowed to happen again. Grant was cautiously confident that he had Lee where he wanted him; still, he later wrote, "I was afraid every morning that I would wake from my sleep to hear that Lee had gone, and that nothing was left but his picket line."[14]

No matter what Lee attempted, the generals agreed that there would be at least "one more desperate and bloody battle." Wringing his hands, Lincoln asked, "Must more blood be shed? Cannot this bloody battle be avoided?" When he was told that was not likely, Lincoln exclaimed, "My God, my God! Can't you spare more effusions of blood? We have had so much of it!"[15]

Lincoln wanted victory won without retribution. He wanted to "defeat the opposing armies, and to get the men composing the Confederate armies back to their homes, at work on their farms and in their shops. Let them have their horses to plow with, and, if you like, their guns to shoot crows with. I want no one punished; treat them liberally all round. We want those people to return to their allegiance to the Union and submit to the laws." Again he emphasized that once the "deluded men of the rebel armies" were allowed to surrender and return to their homes, "they won't take up arms again."[16]

And what of Jefferson Davis, the man so many Northerners wanted to see imprisoned or hanged? Lincoln answered, as he often did, with a humorous story:

A man once had taken the total-abstinence pledge. When visiting a friend, he was invited to take a drink, but declined, on the score of his pledge; when the [friend] suggested lemonade, [the man] accepted. When preparing the lemonade, the friend pointed to the brandy-bottle, and said the lemonade would be more palatable if he were to pour in a little brandy; when his guest said, if he could do so "unbeknown" to him, he would not object.

Sherman took the point of the story immediately. Lincoln "would not object" if Davis and his political cohorts were to "escape the country unbeknown to him."[17]

It seemed to Admiral Porter that Lincoln "wanted peace on almost any terms."[18] But Porter was mistaken. Lincoln would not agree to peace without assurances of Union, emancipation, and (at least limited) equality. When advised that Lee had made recent overtures to Grant, requesting an "interchange of views" on "the subjects of controversy between the belligerents," Lincoln stated firmly that peace negotiations were to be left to him. "Such questions," Lincoln said, "the President holds in his own hands, and will submit them to no military conferences or conventions."[19]

This round of conferences concluded, Sherman and Grant prepared to return to their commands for the expected final assaults. Both generals were impressed with Lincoln's style and convictions. Sherman later wrote of Lincoln's "kindly nature, his deep and earnest sympathy with the afflictions of the whole people, and his absolute faith in the courage, manliness, and integrity of the armies in the field." Later, when Grant left, Lincoln accompanied him to the railroad station, where "his eyes looked more serious than at any other time since he had visited headquarters; the lines in his face seemed deeper, and the rings under his eyes were a darker hue." As the train pulled away Lincoln saluted the officers and called out, "his voice broken by an emotion he could ill conceal, 'Good-by gentlemen, God bless you all!' "[20]

Still Lincoln did not return to Washington. Instead, he waited at City Point for news of his army's progress. On March 30, Lee sent Major General George Pickett's division to a crossroads called Five Forks, southwest of Petersburg. Pickett commanded some five thousand men—a sizable number, although still a shadow of those who had been slaughtered at Gettysburg—and was now instructed to hold the area at all cost, lest Grant gain control of the Southside Railroad line. Grant sent General Sheridan to meet the rebels in torrential rain. "I am ready to strike,"

Sheridan brashly stated, "and go to smashing things!" With the assistance of Brigadier Generals Joshua Chamberlain and George Custer, Sheridan was true to his word, furiously attacking Pickett's forces, inflicting thousands of casualties, and taking scores of prisoners. The crushing defeat of Pickett's division at Five Forks—the historian Bruce Catton called it "*the* great, decisive victory of the whole Civil War"—came to be known as "the Waterloo of the Confederacy."[21]

Now, on Sunday, April 2, the final assault on Petersburg began. Grant's army, which numbered nearly a hundred thousand men, twice the size of Lee's forces, had been waiting for this moment for many months. Both armies fought savagely, but Lee's lines could not withstand the series of coordinated direct assaults. Within hours the centers of the Confederate lines, nicknamed Fort Hell and Fort Damnation, had fallen. As Union flags were unfurled at the siege works, Lee prepared to abandon the city, and that night he took what was left of his forces and looked to escape to the west, along the Appomattox River. Throughout the day, from the deck of the *River Queen*, Lincoln watched the flash of cannon fire from Petersburg.

In Richmond, Jefferson Davis was attending church services when he received Lee's message advising him to evacuate the city. He did so immediately, taking his cabinet westward to Danville, Virginia, and then to Greensboro, North Carolina, on the only available railroad line. Confederate troops fled as well, destroying bridges and burning armories and warehouses as they left. Union soldiers, including some companies of African Americans, quickly stormed in and worked feverishly to put out the fires, but the blazes all but consumed the city. When word of Richmond's fall reached Washington, thousands of people ran into the streets, "talking, laughing, hurrahing, and shouting in the fullness of their joy."[22] Celebratory crowds gathered in front of the War Department and called for Stanton to speak; he was so happy that his voice trembled and his body shook. He expressed his gratitude to "an Almighty God" and "to the President," and then led the throng in singing "The Star-Spangled Banner."[23] Newspapers rushed to print special editions of the news, and that night the capital was alive with fireworks, brass bands, and cannon salutes.

Lincoln found his own way to celebrate. On Tuesday, April 4, he disregarded Stanton's cautionary advice—"I will take care of myself," he said—and went to Richmond to see the former capital city of the Confederacy. Walking two miles from the pier to the center of the smoldering city, Lincoln was met by hundreds of jubilant African Americans as sullen white residents drew their curtains and remained indoors. "From the colored population of Richmond," said a Union officer who accompanied the president, "we received such a reception as could only come from a people who were returning thanks for the deliverance of their race." Crowds of black men, women, and children surrounded him, shouting "Bless the Lord, Father Abraham's come."[24] Some knelt to Lincoln, but he would have none of it. "Don't kneel to me," he said. "You must kneel to God only and thank Him for your freedom."[25] Lincoln made his way to the Confederate White House and sat in Jefferson Davis's chair. Major General Godfrey Weitzel, who now made his headquarters in the house, asked Lincoln how best to handle the people of Richmond. "If I were in your place, I'd let 'em up easy, let 'em up easy," Lincoln said.[26]

Phil Sheridan had no intention of allowing Lee to escape. He caught up with the rear of Lee's army at Saylor's Creek, fifty miles west of Petersburg. Combining with Major General Horatio Wright, Sheridan met some initial resistance from Major Robert Stiles's forces, but within a day the Union's overwhelming numbers resulted in the surrender of eight thousand rebels, or nearly one-fourth of Lee's army. Sheridan telegraphed Grant, "If the thing is pressed, I think Lee will surrender." Lincoln read the forwarded message and replied, "Let the *thing* be pressed."[27]

Lee desperately needed provisions for his starving, exhausted soldiers. He pushed on, hoping to find supplies at the Appomattox station of the Southside Railroad. But Sheridan's hard-riding cavalry arrived first, took control of the station, and skirmished briefly with the dejected Confederates. Surrender was Lee's only realistic option. Though he said he would "rather die a thousand deaths," Lee agreed to meet Grant at the village of Appomattox Court House on Sunday, April 9. Lee was relieved and grateful when Grant offered generous terms: all soldiers, including officers, could return to their homes "not to be disturbed by the United States authority so long as they observe their paroles and the laws in force where they may reside."[28] Though they had to turn in their arms and military equipment, the rebels could keep their horses and could help themselves to twenty-five thousand Union rations. In contrast to four years of bitter, vicious fighting, the surrender was marked by civility and honor. In effect, the war was finally over; although some Confederate forces continued to fight, within two months all hostilities had ceased.

At the same time as Lee and Grant met at Appomattox, Lincoln was on board the *River Queen*, heading up the Potomac toward Washington. News of the surrender arrived around 10 P.M., and the next day the entire city turned out in celebration. Gideon Welles wrote, "The nation seems delirious with joy. Guns are firing, bells ringing, flags flying, men laughing, children cheering— all, all jubilant."[29] The Capitol dome was brilliantly lit, and across the river, at the former home of Robert E. Lee, thousands of freedmen gathered to sing "The Year of Jubilee."[30] Appearing briefly at a White House window, Lincoln asked that the band play "Dixie."

During the evening of Tuesday, April 11, Lincoln made his final public address to a crowd gathered on the White House lawn. While many expected a speech of triumph and celebration, Lincoln spoke instead of reconstruction, "restoring the proper practical relations between these states and the Union." He outlined a flexible program, with different approaches for the different states (some of which had been under federal control for two years), and, to appease the radicals, the role Congress might play. He asked Edwin Stanton to draft a plan for military governments in states where anti-Union fervor still ran high. Lincoln also endorsed, for the first time, limited black suffrage. In the crowd, a handsome young actor and Confederate sympathizer named John Wilkes Booth heard those words and said to an associate, "That means nigger citizenship. That is the last speech he will ever make. By God, I'll put him through."[31]

· · ·

Lincoln had been dealing with death for most of his life. He lost his mother and sister when he was still a boy. His first love, Ann Rutledge, died when she was just twenty-two. Two of his four sons, Eddie and Willie, died at early ages. And, of course, hundreds of thousands of Americans lost their lives in the war. Lincoln became emotionally reserved. "If he had griefs," said a friend, "he never spoke of them in general conversation."[32] He was fatalistic about his own death. In 1863 he told the author Harriet Beecher Stowe, "I shan't last long after the war is over." He regularly received death threats, which he shrugged off. Sometimes Lincoln dreamed of death. Soon after Appomattox he told Mary that he dreamed the president had been assassinated.

The last full day of Lincoln's life was Good Friday, April 14, 1865. He was happier that day than he had been in a long time. "His whole appearance, poise, and bearing had marvelously changed," remembered Senator Harlan. "He seemed the very personification of supreme satisfaction. His conversation was, of course, correspondingly exhilarating."[33] Mary joined him for an afternoon carriage ride, and she later noted that he seemed "cheerful—almost joyous." He had a good reason to be in such good spirits, he told her. "I consider this day, the war has come to a close. We must both be more cheerful in the future." They spoke of someday traveling to Europe, and to California, and of returning home to Illinois.

That evening the Lincolns went to Ford's Theatre, on Tenth Street just six blocks from the White House, to see a farce called *Our American Cousin*. Lincoln loved the theater—Shakespearean comedies and tragedies were his favorites—and had seen more than a hundred performances during his tenure as president. General and Mrs. Grant, among others, turned down the Lincolns' invitation to attend the play, but they found a willing couple in Major Henry Rathbone and his fiancée, Clara Harris, the daughter of a New York senator. The party arrived at the theater at about 8:30, and as they made their way to the presidential box, the orchestra played "Hail to the Chief" while the audience stood.

The Lincolns thoroughly enjoyed the play, and each other's company. Mary nestled against her husband and they held hands, laughing and teasing. "What will Miss Harris think of my hanging onto you so?" Mary whispered. Smiling, Lincoln told her, "She won't think anything about it." Meanwhile, John Wilkes Booth steadied his nerves with brandy at a tavern next door and kept his eyes on the clock.

Shortly after ten o'clock, while the play was in its third act, Booth entered the front of the theater. He ascended the stairs to the second level, where several members of the audience noticed him walk down the aisle, behind the dress circle, to the presidential box. He showed his calling card and was allowed inside. A few moments later, as the audience laughed at a humorous line, Booth pointed his derringer at the back of Lincoln's head and fired. Fighting off Major Rathbone's attempts to stop him, Booth jumped to the stage some twelve feet below and shouted the state motto of Virginia, *Sic semper tyrannis*—"Thus always to tyrants." Mary screamed in horror, again and again, as the entire theater, at once confused, terrified, and outraged, erupted in pandemonium. His ankle broken from the fall, Booth scurried off the stage and out the back exit to an alley where his horse waited, and within moments he was galloping away into the foggy Washington night.

A doctor in attendance examined the unconscious Lincoln

and probed the wound, finding the bullet hole and surmising that the ball was lodged behind his right eye. His body was carried across the street to the home of William Petersen and placed on a bed in a small room at the rear of the first floor. Other physicians now arrived on the scene, including Lincoln's family doctor and the surgeon general of the United States; all agreed that the wound was fatal and that the president had but a few hours to live.

Edwin Stanton arrived and immediately took charge, interviewing witnesses and conducting a preliminary investigation. He soon learned that William Seward, resting at his home that evening after a serious carriage accident, had been attacked by an accomplice of Booth's named Lewis Powell. Stanton acted quickly, issuing warrants of arrest and ordering that all bridges and roads leading out of the capital be closed. By dawn a massive manhunt for Booth and Powell was under way.

Soon Robert Lincoln arrived at the Petersen house, as did senators, congressmen, and cabinet members. While Gideon Welles, among others, kept vigil alongside Lincoln's bed, Mary sobbed uncontrollably in the front room. Several times it seemed that Lincoln stopped his labored breathing, and Mary was allowed in, where she kissed him and called him "every endearing name."[34] And several times Lincoln seemed to rally, keeping impossible hopes faintly alive.

He breathed his last at 7:22 on the morning of April 15. "Now he belongs to the ages," said Stanton in a final salute. A minister offered a brief prayer, and one of the physicians informed Mary, "The President is no more."[35] He was fifty-six years of age.

It is one of the cruel paradoxes of American history that Abraham Lincoln, whose heart was filled with compassion and love for his nation and his fellow human beings, North and South, should have been killed by a man whose soul was filled with hate in a theater loved by both the killer and his victim. The larger paradox is that a man who longed for peace and goodwill was called to preside during his days in the White House over one of the bloodiest and most destructive wars in human history. But perhaps the greatest of our presidents would have confronted such puzzling paradoxes in the words he had invoked on other occasions: "The Almighty has his own purposes."

Epilogue

The Nation Lincoln Made

when he shall die,
Take him and cut him out in little stars,
And he will make the face of heaven so fine,
That all the world shall be in love with night.

—William Shakespeare, *Romeo and Juliet*

The death of Abraham Lincoln by an assassin's bullet engulfed the nation in sorrow. The exultation of just days before, wrote one reporter, was now "exchanged for boundless grief."[1] The war itself had not been atonement enough for the nation's sins, many believed. Now, for the first time in the history of the Republic, a president had been killed while in office. On April 18, a procession of twenty-five thousand people viewed Lincoln's body at the White House, the coffin resting on a magnificent catafalque called the "Temple of Death." A military funeral was held in the East Room, attended by six hundred government and military officials; Mary remained upstairs, however, too distraught to attend. Lincoln's pastor, Dr. Phineas Gurley, gave the funeral sermon. "It was a cruel, cruel hand," he said, that dark hand of the assassin, which smote our honored, wise, and noble President, and filled the land with sorrow. But above and beyond that hand is another which we must see and acknowledge. It is the chastening hand of a wise and faithful Father. He has given us this bitter cup. And the cup that our Father has given us, shall we not drink it? . . . Though our beloved President is slain, our beloved country is saved. And so we sing of mercy as well as of judgment. Tears of gratitude mingle with those of sorrow. While there is darkness, there is also the dawning of a brighter, happier day upon our stricken and weary land. God be praised that our fallen Chief lived long enough to see the day dawn and the daystar of joy and peace arise upon the nation. He saw it, and he was glad.[2]

Dr. E. H. Gray, the chaplain of the Senate, closed with a prayer for peace and justice. Across the nation some twenty-five million people attended services with similar messages.

A day later, as church bells tolled and bands played dirges, forty thousand mourners followed the fourteen-foot-long hearse down Pennsylvania Avenue to the Capitol Rotunda. Leading the procession was the same detachment of black soldiers that had been the first to occupy Richmond. Behind the hearse came Lincoln's favorite horse, riderless, Lincoln's boots reversed in the stirrups. Next came a carriage holding Robert and Tad, and then General Grant and cabinet members, clergymen, marshals, and twenty-two honorary pallbearers. Following were waves of military units, all marching to the slow cadence of muffled drums. Hundreds of convalescent soldiers, many on crutches, hobbled along as best they could or stood at attention on the curbs. From the windows and rooftops of homes, shops, and offices, mourners watched solemnly, tearfully, their mood black as the festoons that hung from government buildings. Perhaps most impressively, four thousand African American residents of Washington, wearing high silk hats and white gloves, held hands and walked side by side to the Capitol.

Lincoln lay in state in the Rotunda for twenty-four hours as tens of thousands of people filed past the open coffin to pay their last respects. On Friday morning, April 21, one week after his murder, Lincoln's body was placed on a funeral train that took him, along with the disinterred remains of his son Willie, on a seventeen-hundred-mile journey back to Springfield. The train essentially retraced Lincoln's route of 1861, when he had come to Washington for his first inauguration, passing through Baltimore, Philadelphia, New York, Cleveland, Chicago, and other places. There were twenty cities in all, twenty solemn processions, and twenty funerals. By May 4, when Lincoln was at last entombed at Springfield's Oak Ridge Cemetery, some one million people had said their final good-byes.

· · ·

At length the nation's grief gave way to reverence, and sorrow gave way to esteem. No sooner had Lincoln been laid to rest, no sooner had the conspirators who brought about his death been caught and punished, no sooner had the new president begun to feel the monumental weight that now rested on his shoulders than the nation began to understand just what it had lost. Not since Washington, perhaps, or Jefferson, had the country been led by such a man. He was Honest Abe, a modern-day Moses, the Great Emancipator, Father Abraham. What other person could have guided America through the storm of civil war? Americans had come to rely on Lincoln, Walt Whitman thought, and his "idiomatic western genius." "Jesus Christ died for the world," said a New York minister. "Abraham Lincoln died for his country."[3] In life he was underappreciated and often misunderstood. In death he was transformed to martyr, to legend, and to myth. The transformation continues to this day.

Lincoln had always possessed a powerful ambition. He sensed

it from his earliest years, when he realized that he could do better—that he *had* to do better—than carve a living out of hard-scrabble farming. Embarrassed by his lack of schooling, he took on the task of educating himself. He tried his hand at a variety of positions in New Salem, but always his ambition drove him further ahead. Eventually he found intellectual fulfillment as an attorney, an occupation that allowed him to stretch his mind and match his wits with other learned men. And then he found an outlet for his considerable talents in politics, where he could not only polish his oratorical skills but organize and lead those of similar feelings on questions of the day.

But politics was more than a vehicle for Lincoln to fulfill his personal and professional objectives. He dedicated his efforts not just to gain higher office but to benefit the greater good as well. His purpose in public life, always, was to assist and promote the interests of his fellow humans. He worked on behalf of his constituency, his state, his country. Though his political party changed, he did not waver from some of the key Whig principles that inspired him—the "Great American System" of governmental support for industry, commerce, internal improvements, and education. Lincoln aspired to political greatness, framing everything he did as a statesman with an eye to posterity.[4]

He believed in meritocracy, the idea that all Americans should have the opportunity to prove themselves, to fulfill their own potential as he had done. True equality meant that every American should have the same chance to drink "from the cup of liberty." An American, to Lincoln, was simply a citizen who, regardless of ancestry or race or station in life, believed in the democratic principles upon which the Republic was founded. The promise of the Declaration of Independence—that all men are created equal—was "the father of all moral principle." It represented the idea that fairness and justice must govern relations between government and citizens.

Speaking at Independence Hall in Philadelphia on February

22, 1861, Lincoln told his listeners: "I have never had a feeling politically that did not spring from the sentiments embodied in the Declaration of Independence." Lincoln, of course, had great respect for the Constitution and the Bill of Rights, but it was the Declaration of Independence, with Jefferson's soaring rhetoric, that most stirred his heart and patriotic zeal. He saw the Declaration as a charter of liberty for all humanity. Jefferson authored the sentiment; Lincoln demanded that it be given true meaning.

He was willing to compromise with the slave states but never wavered in his determination to block the extension of slavery into the territories. His refusal to recognize the right of secession of any state was matched by his determination to prevent the spread of slavery. Save the Union, yes, by all means. But that Union must include *liberty for all*.

Coming to Washington in 1861, he was determined to preserve the Union. Every president exercises great power and expects to do great things. But no other president faced the challenges Lincoln faced. He successfully gauged Northern popular sentiment, that secession—the essence of anarchy, he called it—was an indignation that could not be allowed to stand. He had great confidence in the American people. Indeed, he believed that the Unionists in the South would convince their hotheaded friends that secession was a misguided reaction to political dissatisfaction. Ultimately he recognized that loyalists were the government's greatest asset, and that through their sustained effort the rebels would be defeated. The great powers—the unprecedented powers—he exhibited as a war president depended ultimately on public support and justification, on his "harnessing the potent force of popular nationalism."[5] And, he asked, "Why should there not be a patient confidence in the ultimate justice of the people? Is there any better, or equal, hope in the world?"[6]

Lincoln did not start the war. Faced with the choice between disunion and war, he chose the latter. But once begun, he vowed to finish it, and on his terms. There would be no compromise and no negotiation. He remained focused on carrying out his two most important goals: the preservation of the Union and the elimination of slavery. He seized the historic moment, as the historian Richard Carwardine wrote, "as an instrument of a providential purpose."[7] For what began as a war to preserve the Union (and in fact always remained so) became something else as well: a war for human dignity, for equality, for the freedom of an entire race of Americans. His vision was that the promise of the Declaration of Independence should finally be fulfilled. The great patriots of the Revolution had won freedom for America; now would come freedom for all Americans.

At Gettysburg, Lincoln made this clear. The brave men, "these honored dead" who had given "the last full measure of devotion," must not have died in vain. It was "for us the living" to carry on the "unfinished work," the "great task remaining before us." That task was nothing more than a second Revolution, "a new birth of freedom" to shine as a beacon to the whole world.

The war that Lincoln fought gave rise to a new definition of liberty. Prior to the Civil War, liberty was thought to be the restraint of government from tyrannizing the individual. After the war, liberty was something that the government helped to provide; it was the broadening of individual empowerment (particularly, of course, for blacks). The historian James McPherson points out that this redefinition of liberty, and of the role the government must play in fostering it, was a direct result of Lincoln's recognition that the abolition of slavery had to become a war aim if the promise of the first American Revolution was to be fulfilled.[8]

Through war, the union of states became a nation. Gone forever was the South's concept of the Republic: a government of limited powers that worked primarily to protect (white) property owners, and a social order predicated on family, kinship, and tradition. In its place came a strong centralized government that promoted industrial development, competition, and free-labor capitalism. Government would go on to play a much more significant role in the lives of average Americans, as evidenced by the national Constitution itself. Eleven of the first twelve amendments to the Constitution limited the powers of the national government; after 1865, six of the next seven amendments expanded those powers, always with a lesser governing role for the states.

. . .

What can be gained from further study of Lincoln's life and times? How does he inspire us today?

In Lincoln we see what is possible. We look to the humble circumstances of his birth, the disappointments that marked his middle years, and the unlikely rise from relative obscurity to presidential power. He struggled through his prejudices and emerged a better man. From reasoned, sober introspection he found a strength and determination that enabled him to overcome repeated disappointment. There was no time to lose faith in himself. He took solace in his family and he believed in the sanctity of the institutions in which he toiled. He asked profound questions. He was determined to leave the world a better place for his existence. He worked, every day, to fulfill his potential. We examine his life and we wonder what we can make of our own.

In Lincoln we see the essence of leadership. He inspired a people and an army by steady, measured resolve. He mobilized and energized the nation by appealing to the best and highest of ideals; that is, he convinced the nation that "a more perfect Union"—a Union of justice and freedom—was worth fighting for.

He grew, sometimes painfully, with the task before him. He was not afraid to acknowledge his mistakes. Perseverance was his greatest asset; from "noble effort," one biographer noted, came "great strength."[9] He spoke beautifully, sometimes majestically. It is doubtful that we have ever had a president who cared so much about every single word he spoke or wrote. In eulogizing Henry Clay he might have been describing himself: "He did not consist of . . . elegant arrangements of words and sentences; but rather of that deeply earnest and impassioned tone, and manner, which can proceed only from great sincerity and a thorough conviction . . . of the justice and importance of the cause."[10]

In Lincoln we see the decency of popular government. Its role, then as now, was "to elevate the condition of men . . . to afford all, an unfettered start, in the race of life." The war was a "People's contest," he said, because upon its outcome depended the proposition that the will of the majority must prevail. To him democracy was an experiment that the world had not seen before; it had been successfully established and administered, but now it had to be maintained against "a formidable attempt to overthrow it." Lincoln knew that other nations were watching events in America closely, and anxiously. America's promise of life, liberty, and the pursuit of happiness was nothing less than the hope of the world.[11]

In Lincoln we see the challenge for the future. He passed from life to history, but the history was, and is, ours to make.[12] He wished for the "kindly spirit" of America, "a Union of hearts and hands as well as of States."[13] He knew that America had a destiny to fulfill: true democracy, where man is neither master nor slave; equality for all, the "central idea" of the Republic; and liberty, the cause of which "must not be surrendered at the end of *one*, or even one *hundred* defeats."[14] Since Lincoln's time there have been many defeats, but many more victories. The "better angels of our nature" still guide us as we struggle to achieve democracy, equality, and liberty. Lincoln's life, and his death, gave Americans a new impulse of patriotism—of love of country—that reverberates today.

. . .

Abraham Lincoln is revered throughout the world, but he is, of course, particularly celebrated in America. For 150 years every schoolchild has learned the lessons of his life. Lincoln saved the Union. He freed the slaves. He went from a log cabin to the White House. He knew the difference between right and wrong. He was not perfect, but he was a good man, kind and honest, simple in his tastes, magnanimous in his feeling. He won the war and then looked to welcome erring brothers back into the fold of America.

Abraham Lincoln holds the highest place in American history. General William T. Sherman said, "Of all the men I ever met, he seemed to possess more of the elements of greatness, combined with goodness, than any other."[15] He was our greatest president, against whom all others will forever be measured. We wish our leaders could be more like him; we wish we all could be. There has never been an American story like Abraham Lincoln's.

Notes

PROLOGUE: THE GREATNESS OF LINCOLN

1. Richard Carwardine, *Lincoln: A Life of Purpose and Power*, pp. 1–6.
2. Joshua Wolf Shenk, *Lincoln's Melancholy: How Depression Challenged a President and Fueled His Greatness*, p. 4.
3. Ibid., p. 5.
4. Ibid., pp. 22–23.
5. Ibid., p. 56.
6. Merrill D. Peterson, *Lincoln in American Memory*, p. 31.
7. Peterson, p. 32.
8. Mark E. Neely Jr., *The Lincoln Administration and Arbitrary Arrests: A Reconsideration*, paper presented at the Louis A. Warren Lincoln Library and Museum at the Abraham Lincoln Symposium, 1983.
9. Ibid.
10. Dinesh D'Souza, "Why He's Called Honest" (review of *Lincoln's Virtues* by William L. Miller), *Los Angeles Times*, February 17, 2002.
11. Robert Saladin, abstract, White House Studies, vol. 4, no. 4, p. 487.
12. Peterson, p. 31.

1. HUMBLE BEGINNINGS

1. David Herbert Donald, Lincoln, p. 28.
2. William E. Gienapp, *Abraham Lincoln and Civil War America*, p. 5.
3. Ibid., p. 7.

4. Ibid.
5. Ibid., p. 13.
6. Ibid., p. 14.
7. Larry D. Mansch, *Abraham Lincoln, President-Elect*, p. 17.
8. Gienapp, p. 16.
9. Kenneth J. Winkle, *The Young Eagle: The Rise of Abraham Lincoln*, p. 75.
10. Mansch, p. 18.
11. Ibid., p. 20.
12. Ibid.
13. Ibid., p. 24.
14. Shenk, pp. 19–22.
15. Ibid., p. 21.
16. Donald, pp. 63–64.
17. Ibid., p. 24.
18. Ibid., p. 84.
19. Mansch, p. 27.
20. Ibid.
21. Mansch, ibid.; Shenk, pp. 49–58.
22. Shenk, p. 57.
23. Ibid.
24. Ibid.

2. THE MAKING OF A STATESMAN

1. Donald, p. 129.
2. Stephen B. Oates, *With Malice Toward None: A Life of Abraham Lincoln*, p. 52.
3. Joel H. Silbey, "Always a Whig in Politics: The Partisan Life of Abraham Lincoln," *Journal of the Abraham Lincoln Association*, vol. 8, no. 1 (1986).
4. Donald, p. 111.
5. Richard J. Carwardine, "Lincoln, Evangelical Religion, and American Political Culture in the Era of the Civil War," *Journal of the Abraham Lincoln Association*, vol. 18, no. 1 (1997).
6. Donald, p. 128.
7. Ibid., p. 135.
8. Mansch, pp. 36–39.
9. John Mack Faragher, Mari Jo Buhle, Daniel Czitrom, and Susan H. Armitage, *Out of Many: A History of the American People*, p. 263.
10. Gienapp, p. 49.
11. Donald, p. 167.
12. Carwardine, *Lincoln*, p. 24.

13. Mansch, p. 42.
14. Letter to Owen Lovejoy, August 11, 1855, in John Nicolay and John Hay, eds., *Complete Works of Abraham Lincoln*, vol. 11, p. 287.
15. Oates, p. 121.
16. Ibid., p. 123.
17. Ibid., p. 130.
18. Ibid.
19. Richard W. Donley and Brian Thornton, *101 Things You Didn't Know About Lincoln*, p. 132.
20. Gienapp, p. 63.
21. Ibid., p. 64.
22. Mansch, pp. 44, 45.
23. Donald, p. 228.
24. Mansch, pp. 46–47.
25. Ibid., pp. 47, 48.

3. LINCOLN AND THE UNION

1. Mario Cuomo and Harold Holzer, eds., *Lincoln on Democracy*, p. 185.
2. Mansch, p. 72.
3. Mansch, ibid.; Oates, p. 187.
4. Gienapp, p. 74.
5. Donald, p. 261.
6. Mansch, p. 81.
7. Orville Vernon Burton, *The Age of Lincoln*, p. 117.
8. Donald, p. 260.
9. Rufus Rockwell Wilson, *Intimate Memories of Lincoln*, p. 503.
10. Gienapp, p. 74.
11. Mansch, p. 171.
12. Cuomo and Holzer, p. 201.
13. Ibid., p. 204.
14. Ibid., p. 205.
15. Ibid.
16. Ibid.
17. Ibid., p. 206.
18. Ibid., pp. 207, 208.
19. Ibid., p. 209.
20. Ibid.
21. Mark E. Neely Jr., *The Abraham Lincoln Encyclopedia*, p. 135, and Neely, *The Fate of Liberty*, pp. 113–38.
22. Ex re Merryman
23. Neely, *Fate of Liberty*, p. 31.
24. Neely, *Abraham Lincoln Encyclopedia*, p. 69.

4. LINCOLN AND EMANCIPATION

1. Speech in Hartford, Connecticut, March 5, 1860, in Roy P. Basler, ed., *The Collected Works of Abraham Lincoln*, vol. 4, p. 2.
2. Allen C. Guelzo, "The Great Event of the Nineteenth Century: Lincoln Issues the Emancipation Proclamation," *Pennsylvania Legacies*, vol. 4, no. 2, November 2004.
3. Letter to Albert G. Hodges, April 4, 1864, in *Collected Works*, vol. 7, p. 282.
4. Ibid., vol. 1, pp. 74–75, March 3, 1837.
5. Cuomo and Holzer, p. 55.
6. Guelzo, p. 131.
7. Quoted in Cuomo and Holzer, p. 74.
8. Donald, pp. 176, 224.
9. Speech at the Freedmen's Monument, April 16, 1876, in Frederick Douglass, *Life and Times of Frederick Douglass*, p. 489.
10. Don E. Fehrenbacher, *Lincoln in Text and Context*, p. 104; Douglass, pp. 485–86 (speech at the Freedmen's Monument, April 16, 1876).
11. Don E. Fehrenbacher, ed., *Abraham Lincoln: Speeches and Writings*, p. 302.
12. Letter to Henry Pierce, April 6, 1859, ibid., p. 19.
13. Doris Kearns Goodwin, *Team of Rivals*, pp. 462–63.
14. *Collected Works*, vol. 5, p. 317.
15. Donald, p. 405.
16. Ibid., p. 463.
17. *Collected Works*, vol. 6, pp. 29–30.
18. James Conkling letter, August 26, 1863, in *Speeches and Writings*, p. 498.
19. Goodwin, p. 468.
20. Ibid., p. 469.
21. Ibid., p. 471.
22. Jefferson Davis, message to Confederate Congress, January 12, 1863; Richmond *Examiner*, January 13, 1863.
23. Richard Striner, *Father Abraham: Lincoln's Relentless Struggle to End Slavery*, p. 2.
24. Letter to Hodges, in *Collected Works*, pp. 281–82.
25. Ralph Waldo Emerson, "The President's Proclamation," *Atlantic Monthly*, vol. 10, no. 61, November 1862, pp. 638–42.
26. Peterson, p. 29.
27. James M. McPherson, *Battle Cry of Freedom: The Civil War Era*, p. 564.
28. John Y. Simon, Harold Holzer, and William D. Pederson, eds., *Lincoln Forum: Lincoln, Gettysburg and the Civil War*, p. 57.

29. Don E. Fehrenbacher and Virginia E. Fehrenbacher, eds., *Recollected Words of Abraham Lincoln*, p. 413.

5. LINCOLN AND TOTAL WAR

1. Russell Frank Weigley, *A Great Civil War: A Military and Political History, 1861–1865*, p. 93.
2. Gienapp, p. 100.
3. Ibid., p. 99.
4. Ibid., p. 100.
5. Richard N. Current, *The Lincoln Nobody Knows*, p. 138.
6. Gienapp, p. 101.
7. Ibid.
8. *Collected Works*, vol. 5, p. 223.
9. Neely, p. 151.
10. Gienapp, p. 138.
11. James M. McPherson, *This Mighty Scourge: Perspectives on the Civil War*, p. 126.
12. Gienapp, p. 159.
13. McPherson, *This Mighty Scourge*, p. 126.
14. Shelby Foote, *The Civil War, A Narrative: Fort Sumter to Perryville*, p. 529.
15. Stephen B. Oates, *Abraham Lincoln: The Man Behind the Myth*, p. 134.
16. Gienapp, p. 161.
17. McPherson, *This Mighty Scourge*, p. 124.
18. Sherman, *Memoirs*, p. 589.
19. Ibid.
20. Henry Hitchcock, *Marching with Sherman: Passages from the Letters and Campaign Diaries of Henry Hitchcock, Major and Assistant Adjutant General of Volunteers, November 1864–May 1865*, ed. M. A. DeWolfe Howe, p. 125.
21. McPherson, *This Mighty Scourge*, p. 128.
22. T. Harry Williams, "The Military Leadership of the North and South," in David Donald, ed., *Why the North Won the Civil War*, pp. 43–44.
23. William C. Carter, ed., *Conversations with Shelby Foote*, p. 173.
24. James Ford Rhodes, *Lectures on the American Civil War*, p. 99.

6. POLITICS IN WARTIME

1. Larry T. Balsamo, "We Cannot Have Free Government Without Elections": Abraham Lincoln and the Election of 1864," *Journal of the Illinois State Historical Society*, Summer 2001; Russell L. Riley, *The Presidency and the Power of Racial Inequality*, p. 100.

2. T. Harry Williams, *Lincoln and the Radicals*, p. 310.

3. John C. Waugh, *Reelecting Lincoln: The Battle for the 1864 Presidency*, pp. 38, 112.

4. Ibid., p. 38.

5. Ibid.

6. Ibid., p. 115.

7. Ibid., p. 122.

8. Ibid., p. 124.

9. Ibid.

10. *Speeches and Writings*, p. 599.

11. Balsamo, p. 6.

12. *Speeches and Writings*, p. 601.

13. Balsamo, p. 7.

14. Waugh, p. 31.

15. Balsamo, p. 10.

16. Hans L. Trefousse, *First Among Equals: Abraham Lincoln's Reputation During His Administration*, p. 110.

17. Phillip Shaw Paludan, *The Presidency of Abraham Lincoln*, p. 289.

18. Ibid., p. 285.

7. RISING ABOVE THE FRAY: SECOND TERM

1. Oates, *With Malice Toward None*, p. 402.

2. Goodwin, p. 669.

3. Ibid., p. 578.

4. Ibid., p. 745.

5. Ibid.

6. Ibid.

7. Ibid., p. 672.

8. Ibid., p. 676.

9. Ibid., p. 680.

10. *Speeches and Writings*, pp. 646–61.

11. Thomas F. Schwartz, *For a Vast Future Also*: *Essays from the Journal of the Abraham Lincoln Association*, p. 23; Goodwin, p. 686.

12. Michael Vorenberg, *Final Freedom: The Civil War, the Abolition of Slavery, and the Thirteenth Amendment*, p. 180; Richard Striner, *Father Abraham: Lincoln's Relentless Struggle to End Slavery*, p. 247.

13. Goodwin, p. 689.

14. Ibid.

15. Ibid.

16. Oates, *With Malice Toward None*, p. 405.

17. Goodwin, p. 690.

18. William Charles Harris, *Lincoln's Last Months*, p. 133.

8. VICTORY AND DEATH

1. Geoffrey C. Ward, with Ric Burns and Ken Burns, *The Civil War*, p. 319.
2. Ibid., pp. 409–10.
3. Oates, *With Malice Toward None*, p. 409.
4. Goodwin, p. 702.
5. Ward, p. 360.
6. Shenk, pp. 196–99.
7. *Speeches and Writings*, pp. 686–87.
8. Donald, p. 568.
9. Ibid.
10. Neil Kagan, ed., *Eyewitness to the Civil War: The Complete History from Secession to Reconstruction*, p. 356.
11. Goodwin, p. 709.
12. Ibid., p. 710.
13. Gienapp, p. 196.
14. Kagan, p. 364.
15. Jay Winik, *April 1865: The Month That Saved America*, p. 67.
16. Goodwin, p. 713.
17. Ibid.
18. Winik, p. 68.
19. Donald, p. 573.
20. Ibid., p. 714.
21. Bruce Catton, "Sheridan at Five Forks," *Journal of Southern History*, vol. 21, no. 5, August 1955, p. 305; Kagan, pp. 365–66.
22. Goodwin, p. 717.
23. Ibid.
24. Donald, p. 576.
25. Kagan, p. 370.
26. Ibid., p. 371.
27. Ibid., p. 373.
28. Ibid.
29. Goodwin, p. 726.
30. Donald, p. 581.
31. Gienapp, p. 200; Goodwin, p. 728.
32. Shenk, pp. 107–8.
33. Donald, p. 593.
34. Ibid., p. 599.
35. Ibid.

EPILOGUE: THE NATION LINCOLN MADE

1. Champ Clark, ed., *The Assassination*, p. 119.
2. Dorothy Meserve Kunhardt and Philip B. Kunhardt Jr., *Twenty Days*, p. 128; and see http://showcase.netins.net/web/creative/lincoln/speeches/gurley.htm.
3. Oates, *Abraham Lincoln: The Man Behind the Myth*, p. 4.
4. See Kenneth L. Deutsch and Joseph E. Forniere, eds., *Lincoln's American Dreams: Clashing Political Perspectives*.
5. Carwardine, *Lincoln*, p. 319.
6. *Speeches and Writings*, p. 223.
7. Carwardine, *Lincoln*, p. 314.
8. See James McPherson, *Battle Cry of Freedom: The Civil War Era*.
9. Benjamin P. Thomas, *Abraham Lincoln*, p. 496.
10. Cuomo and Holzer, p. xxxiii.
11. Ibid., pp. 267–69.
12. Carwardine, *Lincoln*, p. 326.
13. Cuomo and Holzer, p. 349.
14. Ibid., p. 136.
15. Goodwin, p. 713.

Milestones

1809   Abraham Lincoln born in log cabin on Nolin Creek in Kentucky on February 12.

1816   Lincoln family relocates to backwoods of Indiana.

1818   Abraham's mother, Nancy Hanks Lincoln, dies October 5 of "milk sickness."

1819   Thomas Lincoln, Abraham's father, marries Sarah Bush Johnston, for whom Abraham has great affection. She promotes his love of learning.

1828   During a trip to New Orleans, Lincoln observes a slave auction, which leads to his lifelong revulsion of slavery.

1831   Lincoln settles in New Salem, Illinois, where he helps run a general store, works as a clerk on the local election board, joins the town's debating society, and performs odd jobs for the townspeople.

1832   Black Hawk War breaks out and Lincoln enlists but doesn't fight in battle. Becomes a candidate for the Illinois General Assembly but loses the election.

1833   Lincoln and a partner acquire a store in New Salem that fails, leaving him in debt; appointed deputy county surveyor.

1834	Elected at age twenty-five to the Illinois General Assembly as a member of the Whig Party.
1835	Lincoln falls in love with Ann Rutledge, but she dies of typhoid fever.
1836	Reelected to the Illinois General Assembly. Receives law license. Suffers a bout of severe depression.
1838	Reelected to Illinois General Assembly and becomes Whig floor leader.
1839	Travels as a lawyer in central and eastern Illinois. Meets Mary Todd at a dance.
1840	Becomes engaged to Mary Todd.
1841	Breaks off engagement with Mary Todd on January 1 and experiences another bout of depression.
1842	Resumes courtship of Mary Todd and the two marry on November 4.
1843	Unsuccessful in bid for Whig nomination for U.S. congressional seat. First son, Robert Todd Lincoln, is born August 1.
1844	Family moves to Springfield and Lincoln sets up law practice.
1846	Second son, Edward Baker Lincoln, born March 10, and Lincoln is nominated to be Whig candidate for U.S. Congress.
1847	Takes seat as Thirtieth Congress convenes. Questions President James K. Polk's war policy toward Mexico.
1849	Leaves politics and returns to Springfield to practice law.
1850	Son Edward dies February 1. Third son, William Wallace Lincoln, is born December 31. Traveling lawyer in Eighth Judicial Circuit.
1853	Fourth son, Thomas (Tad) Lincoln, born April 4.
1854	Reenters politics and opposes Kansas-Nebraska Act.
1855	Fails to be chosen by the Illinois legislature to run for the U.S. Senate.

1856   Helps organize the new Republican Party.

1857   Speaks out against *Dred Scott* decision June 26 in Springfield.

1858   Nominated to be Republican candidate for U.S. senator from Illinois, opposing Stephen A. Douglas. Series of debates between the candidates. Gives "house divided" speech.

1859   The Illinois legislature chooses Douglas as U.S. senator by a vote of 54 to 46.

1860   Delivers Cooper Union speech ("right makes might") on February 27. Nominated on May 18 to be Republican candidate for president. Elected president on November 6. South Carolina secedes from the Union.

1861   Mississippi, Florida, Alabama, Georgia, Louisiana, and Texas secede. Lincoln delivers first inaugural address on March 4. Civil War begins April 12 when Confederates fire on Fort Sumter in Charleston, South Carolina. Virginia secedes from the Union, followed by North Carolina, Tennessee, and Arkansas. Lincoln authorizes suspension of the writ of habeas corpus. Union defeat at the Battle of Bull Run on July 21. Lincoln appoints George B. McClellan as commander of the Union Army on November 1.

1862   Lincoln's son Willie dies on February 20. Battle of Shiloh with huge losses on both sides on April 6. Lincoln approves Homestead Act on May 20 and a law prohibiting slavery in the territories on June 19. Union victory at Battle of Antietam enables Lincoln to issue preliminary Emancipation Proclamation on September 22.

1863   Lincoln issues Emancipation Proclamation on January 1. Lincoln signs a bill creating a national banking system. Union victories at Gettysburg on July 3 and Vicksburg on July 4. Lincoln delivers Gettysburg Address on November 19.

1864   Appoints Ulysses S. Grant as general-in-chief of all the
          federal armies. William T. Sherman succeeds Grant as
          commander in the West and burns Atlanta on Septem-
          ber 2. Lincoln reelected president. Sherman marches to
          the sea and reaches Savannah on December 20.

1865   Lincoln delivers second inaugural address on March 4.
          Robert E. Lee surrenders to Grant at Appomattox
          Court House, Virginia, on April 9. Lincoln is shot in
          Washington on April 14 by John Wilkes Booth and dies
          the following morning. Lincoln is buried outside
          Springfield, Illinois.

Selected Bibliography

Angle, Paul, ed. *The Lincoln Reader.* New Brunswick, N.J.: Rutgers University Press, 1947.

Balsamo, Larry T. "Abraham Lincoln and the Election of 1864." *Journal of the Illinois State Historical Society,* Summer 2001.

Basler, Roy P., ed. *The Collected Works of Abraham Lincoln.* 9 volumes. Springfield, Ill.: Abraham Lincoln Association, 1953.

Burton, Orville Vernon. *The Age of Lincoln.* New York: Hill and Wang, 2007.

Carter, William C., ed. *Conversations with Shelby Foote.* Jackson, Miss.: University Press of Mississippi, 1989.

Carwardine, Richard. *Lincoln: A Life of Purpose and Power.* New York: Pearson Longman, 2003.

———. "Lincoln, Evangelical Religion, and American Political Culture in the Era of the Civil War." *Journal of the Abraham Lincoln Association,* vol. 18, no. 1, 1997.

Catton, Bruce. "Sheridan at Five Forks." *Journal of Southern History,* vol. 21, no. 5, August 1955.

Clark, Champ, ed. *The Assassination.* New York: Time-Life Books, 1987.

Cuomo, Mario, and Harold Holzer, eds. *Lincoln on Democracy.* New York: HarperCollins, 1990.

Deutsch, Kenneth L., and Joseph E. Forniere, eds. *Lincoln's American Dreams: Clashing Political Perspectives.* Washington, D.C.: Potomac Books, 2005.

Donald, David Herbert. *Lincoln.* London: Jonathan Cape, 1997.

Donley, Richard W., and Brian Thornton. *101 Things You Didn't Know*

About Lincoln: Loves and Losses, Political Power Plays, White House Hauntings. Avon, Mass.: Adams Media, 2005.

Douglass, Frederick. *Life and Times of Frederick Douglass: His Early Life As a Slave, His Escape from Bondage, His Complete History to the Present Time.* Digital Scanning, April 2001.

D'Souza, Dinesh. "Why He's Called Honest." *Los Angeles Times*, February 17, 2002.

Faragher, John M., ed. *Out of Many: A History of the American People.* Upper Saddle River, N.J.: Prentice-Hall, 2001.

Fehrenbacher, Don E., ed. *Abraham Lincoln: Speeches and Writings, 1859–1865.* New York: Library of America, 1989.

———. *Lincoln in Text and Context.* Stanford, Calif.: Stanford University Press, 1988.

———, and Virginia E. Fehrenbacher, eds. *Recollected Words of Abraham Lincoln.* Stanford, Calif.: Stanford University Press, 1996.

Foner, Eric. *Free Soil, Free Labor, Free Men: The Ideology of the Republican Party Before the Civil War.* New York: Oxford University Press, 1995.

Foote, Shelby. *The Civil War, A Narrative.* 3 vols. New York: Random House, 1958–1974.

Gienapp, William E. *Abraham Lincoln and Civil War America: A Biography.* New York: Oxford University Press, 2002.

Goodwin, Doris Kearns. *Team of Rivals.* New York: Simon and Schuster, 2005.

Guelzo, Allen C. "The Great Event of the Nineteenth Century: Lincoln Issues the Emancipation Proclamation." *Pennsylvania Legacies*, vol. 4, no. 2, November 2004.

Harris, William Charles. *Lincoln's Last Months.* Cambridge, Mass.: Harvard University Press, 2004.

Hay, John. *Inside Lincoln's White House: The Complete Civil War Diary of John Hay.* Carbondale, Ill.: Southern Illinois University Press, 1997.

Herndon, William Henry. *Herndon's Life of Lincoln.* New York: DaCapo, 1983.

Holt, Michael F. *The Rise and Fall of the American Whig Party: Jacksonian Politics and the Onset of the Civil War.* New York: Oxford University Press, 1999.

Kagan, Neil, ed. *Eyewitness to the Civil War: The Complete History from Secession to Reconstruction.* Washington, D.C.: National Geographic Society, 2006.

Keneally, Thomas. *Abraham Lincoln* (Penguin Lives). New York: Viking, 2002.

Kunhardt, Dorothy Meserve, and Philip B. Kunhardt. *Twenty Days.* New York: HarperCollins, 1993.

Lincoln, Abraham. *The Papers of Abraham Lincoln*. Manuscript Division, Library of Congress, Washington, D.C.

Mansch, Larry D. *Abraham Lincoln, President-Elect: The Four Critical Months from Election*. Jefferson, N.C.: McFarland, 2005.

McPherson, James M. *Battle Cry of Freedom: The Civil War Era*. New York: Oxford University Press, 1988.

———. *Drawn with the Sword: Reflections on the American Civil War*. New York: Oxford University Press, 1997.

———. *This Mighty Scourge: Perspectives on the Civil War*. New York: Oxford University Press, 2007.

Miller, William Lee. *Lincoln's Virtues: An Ethical Biography*. New York: Alfred A. Knopf, 2002.

Mitgang, Herbert. *Abraham Lincoln: A Press Portrait*. New York: Fordham University Press, 2002.

Neely, Mark E., Jr. *The Abraham Lincoln Encyclopedia*. New York: McGraw-Hill, 1981.

———. *The Fate of Liberty: Abraham Lincoln and Civil Liberties*. New York: Oxford University Press, 1991.

Nevins, Allan. *The Emergence of Lincoln*. New York: Scribner's, 1950.

Nicolay, John G. *The Outbreak of Rebellion*. New York: DaCapo, 1995.

Oates, Stephen B. *Abraham Lincoln: Man Behind the Myths*. New York: HarperPerennial, 1994.

———. *With Malice Toward None: A Life of Abraham Lincoln*. New York: HarperCollins, 1994.

Paludan, Phillip Shaw. *The Presidency of Abraham Lincoln*. Lawrence, Kan.: University of Kansas Press, 1994.

Peterson, Merrill D. *Lincoln in American Memory*. New York: Oxford University Press, 1994.

Potter, David M. *Lincoln and His Party in the Secession Crisis*. New Haven: Yale University Press, 1942.

Randall, J. G. *Lincoln the President*. New York: Dodd, Mead, 1945.

Rhodes, James Ford. *Lectures on the American Civil War; Delivered Before the University of Oxford in Easter and Trinity Terms 1912*. Freeport, N. Y.: Books for Libraries Press, 1971.

Riley, Russell L. *The Presidency and the Power of Racial Inequality*. New York: Columbia University Press, 1999.

Saladin, Robert. *White House Studies*, vol. 4, no. 4, abstract.

Sandburg, Carl. *Abraham Lincoln: The Prairie Years and the War Years. 1809–1865*. New York: Dell, 1954.

Schwartz, Thomas F. *For a Vast Future Also: Essays from the Journal of the Abraham Lincoln Association*. New York: Fordham University Press, 1999.

Shenk, Joshua Wolf. *Lincoln's Melancholy: How Depression Challenged a*

President and Fueled His Greatness. Boston: Houghton Mifflin, 2006.

Silbey, Joel H. "Always a Whig in Politics: The Partisan Life of Abraham Lincoln." *Journal of the Abraham Lincoln Association,* vol. 8, no. 1, 1986.

Simon, John Y., Harold Holzer, and William D. Pederson, eds. *Lincoln Forum: Lincoln, Gettysburg and the Civil War.* Cambridge, Mass.: DaCapo Press, 1999.

Striner, Richard. *Father Abraham: Lincoln's Relentless Struggle to End Slavery.* New York: Oxford University Press, 2006.

Thomas, Benjamin P. *Abraham Lincoln.* New York: Alfred A. Knopf, 1952.

Trefousse, Hans L. *First Among Equals: Abraham Lincoln's Reputation During His Administration.* New York: Fordham University Press, 2005.

Vorenberg, Michael. *Final Freedom: The Civil War, the Abolition of Slavery, and the Thirteenth Amendment.* New York: Cambridge University Press, 2001.

Ward, Geoffrey C., with Ric Burns and Ken Burns. *The Civil War.* New York: Alfred A. Knopf, 1990.

Waugh, Jack. *Reelecting Lincoln: The Battle for the 1864 Presidency.* Cambridge, Mass.: DaCapo Press, 1999.

Weigley, Russell Frank. *A Great Civil War: A Military and Political History, 1861–1865.* Bloomington, Ind.: Indiana University Press, 2000.

White, Ronald C. *The Eloquent President: A Portrait of Lincoln Through His Words.* New York: Random House, 2005.

Wilentz, Sean. *The Rise of American Democracy—Jefferson to Lincoln.* New York: W. W. Norton, 2005.

Williams, Thomas Harry. "The Military Leadership of North and South," in David Donald, ed., *Why the Noth Won the Civil War.* New York: Collier Books, 1976.

———. Lincoln and the Radicals. Madison, Wis.: University of Wisconsin Press, 2005.

Wilson, Douglas L. *Lincoln's Sword: The Presidency and the Power of Words.* New York: Alfred A. Knopf, 2006.

Wilson, Rufus Rockwell, ed. *Intimate Memories of Lincoln.* New York: Primavera Press, 1942.

Winik, Jay. *April 1865: The Month That Saved America.* New York: HarperCollins, 2001.

Winkle, Kenneth J. *The Young Eagle: The Rise of Abraham Lincoln.* Dallas, Tex.: Taylor Trade Publishing, 2001.

Acknowledgments

My longtime treasured friend the late Arthur Schlesinger Jr. has placed me in his debt by asking me to write this book about my presidential hero, Abraham Lincoln. I wish that I could have borrowed Arthur's magic pen to do the writing.

Paul Golob of Times Books/Henry Holt has patiently, critically, and helpfully kept me on a steady course from the prologue to the final line. I also deeply appreciate the superb work of the copy editor, Emily DeHuff.

Professor Sean Wilentz of Princeton University, one of America's rising stars in the study and writing of history, has been an ideal replacement for Arthur as the general editor.

I'm deeply indebted to the Montana Lincoln scholar Larry Mansch for his assistance in both the research and the composition of the book.

I would also like to thank the reference staff at the National Reference Center for Bioethics Literature for their assistance in helping me complete the endnotes.

Index

About the Author

GEORGE MCGOVERN represented South Dakota in the United States Senate from 1963 to 1981 and was the Democratic nominee for president in 1972. He was a decorated bomber pilot in World War II, after which he earned his Ph.D. in American history and government at Northwestern University. A recipient of the Presidential Medal of Freedom and the World Food Prize, he lives in Mitchell, South Dakota, and St. Augustine, Florida.